Three Principles of
Angelic Wisdom

Other Books by Linda Pendleton

A Walk Through Grief: Crossing the Bridge Between Worlds

Nonfiction Books by Don and Linda Pendleton

To Dance With Angels
Whispers From the Soul
The Metaphysics of the Novel

Novels by Linda and Don Pendleton

One Dark and Stormy Night…the Search for the Sunrise Killer
Re-titled, *Roulette*

Three Principles of Angelic Wisdom

◆

The Spiritual Psychology of the Grand Spirit, Dr. Peebles

Linda Pendleton

Writers Club Press
New York Lincoln Shanghai

Three Principles of Angelic Wisdom
The Spiritual Psychology of the Grand Spirit, Dr. Peebles

Writers Club Press
an imprint of iUniverse, Inc.

For information address:
iUniverse, Inc.
2021 Pine Lake Road, Suite 100
Lincoln, NE 68512
www.iuniverse.com

Cover Design by Judy Bullard

Previously e-published by Mystic Ink Publishing

ISBN: 0-595-26274-0

Printed in the United States of America

"There is another reality enfolding ours—as close as our breath!"
—Don Pendleton, May, 1995

"Listen for the flutter of an angel's wing as it softly touches you with love. Embrace it and join in the dance!"
—Linda Pendleton, May, 1996

"We dance for you, we entertain you, we give you symphonies of life, and you have every opportunity to be thrilled to the core of your being…but it must be no more or no less than your own free will to translate as you prefer."
—The "spirit" Dr. Peebles
to Don and Linda Pendleton, May, 1987,
To Dance With Angels

"Spirits are but men and women divested of their mortal bodies. They have taken with them consciousness, memory, reason, sympathy, character. They walk by our side often, and yet unseen…There is but one world, and that one world embraces the yesterdays, the todays, and the innumerable tomorrows of eternity."
—Dr. James Martin Peebles, 1910

This book is dedicated with love and blessings to my family, and to the Number One Angel in my life, my late husband, Don Pendleton, who continues to surround me with his love, comfort, and inspiration.

—L.P.

Contents

Acknowledgments

The writing of this book was a wonderfully transformative experience for me personally. The idea for it had been "brewing" in my mind for quite some time before coming into being. I had felt that Dr. Peebles' three principles, which Don and I had introduced in *To Dance With Angels,* and the basis of the Doc's spiritual psychology, were so very important and needed further exploration for readers.

I do believe I was being "pushed gently" from the other side to write the book. I also received encouragement from friends to do so. They, one and all, knew the value of Dr. Peebles' spiritual psychology. Enthusiasm flowed abundantly from Jay Douglas Halford, as it always does when it comes to our friend, Dr. Peebles. Athena Demetrios encouraged and inspired me to move forward with the book and my own channeling of the Doc. Anne Boss was supportive, encouraging, and bubbling with enthusiasm to hear more from Dr. P.

I also want to thank all the others who have shared their connection to Dr. Peebles within the pages of my book: Dr. Fred Bader, Lee Chaifetz, Rhonda Boss, Marie McDaniel, Jery Dickinson, and Nita Reynolds Trocosso. It is great to have good friends like this bunch.

I especially thank Mary Jane Scurlock for her special friendship, guidance, and healing hands and energy. It was especially important to me in getting beyond difficult times.

Thanks to Ron and Lisa Bacon for a great friendship—and support when I need it—and for enjoyable times, great discussions, the best home-cooked meals, and relaxation.

I want to thank Thomas Jacobson for his tremendous work with Dr. Peebles. Without his excellent mediumship most of us on this page would not have come together.

I also want to thank both Athena Demitrios and Summer Bacon for carrying on the spiritual psychology of Dr. Peebles through their mediumship.

Thanks to Judy Bullard, my web designer. She has done a great job of bringing forward my ideas and creating beautiful graphics and book covers. Her artistic ability has given me the opportunity to become visible on a large scale.

A special thanks to my sister and friend, Nancy Tarver, who often becomes my editor. It is great to have someone to run things by.

Thanks to Nora Amrani for her work with spirit, including Dr. Peebles, and for our many, many conversations, usually via email at all hours of the night.

And hugs to my special guides, Dr. Peebles, and my loving husband and soul-mate, Don. You both make life more joyous and fascinating.

—Linda, November 2002

James Martin. Peebles, M.D.

INTRODUCTION

It was on a cool Southern California spring evening in 1987 when my late husband, renowned author, Don Pendleton and I made contact with the world of spirit. That event changed our lives, forevermore.

Through the trance-mediumship of Thomas Jacobson we met Dr. James Martin Peebles in the "flesh." I put the word flesh in quotation marks because Dr. Peebles had shed his flesh sixty five years prior to our meeting. He had died in 1922. As we were to learn, his death changed only the location of his consciousness and personality.

The first meeting we had with the "grand spirit" filled us with awe and wonder. Oh, our healthy skepticism remained, if only for moments, as we sat in the home of a stranger, Thomas Jacobson, and watched and listened to what was transpiring before us. Our skepticism was soon replaced by a knowing that we were communicating with someone beyond *this* physical plane. As Thomas sat in a chair across from us, his breathing and consciousness altered, we were filled with the beauty of the experience. Don and I both saw a white glowing energy that radiated several feet out from and above Thomas. And the words of the spirit entity, who was using the body of Thomas, were filled with wisdom and humor, love and compassion.

What occurred that night was extraordinary and incredible. Thomas did not know us, only by first name, but this beautiful spirit who was speaking with us knew us at a very deep soul level. This went way beyond what a psychic could pull out of the ethers.

Dr. Peebles gave us each a life review, not only of this lifetime, but our past lives, which allowed for a clearer understanding of our present life journey.

Don had asked a question, or I suppose it was really a comment that he had always felt that he had a guardian angel on his shoulder watching over him and "nudging" him in the right direction. Don was thinking not only of his World War II years in intense combat but the direction his life had taken with his writing career. He was forty when he gave up a third-level management position in aerospace to focus full time on his writing. Shortly thereafter, he became a publishing phenomenon with the success of his *Executioner* series of action/adventure novels. I don't think either of us was prepared for the answer from Dr. Peebles. He told Don that yes, he did have an angel on his shoulder, that he was surrounded by many spirit guides—and that Saint Paul worked closely with him, usually in the dream state. I think we both fell off our chairs at that moment. You see, Don did not really agree with a lot of what Saint Paul had to say, and felt that Saint Paul may have been responsible for distorting the basic teachings of Jesus and moving women into a lesser role within the church and society. But yet, Don quoted the words of Saint Paul in almost everything he ever wrote and usually in a positive sense. Dr. Peebles also mentioned the emotional pain Don had endured during his twenties and his religious struggles during that same period of his life. At the age of twelve, Don wanted to be a minister. But the war years changed all that. Only days before his fifteenth birthday in December of 1942, Don fraudulently enlisted in the Navy and when he came out of the service in 1947 he embarked on a struggle with his religious views. He often said he became an agnostic during those years and he was about thirty before he regained a firm spiritual conviction. Dr. Peebles also related how Don was an inspiration to many and how his inspiration allowed others to see how powerful they are, "how large they are." Dr. Peebles' use of the word "large" had special significance. "Live large" was the theme of Don's *Mack Bolan* character in the *Executioner* novels.

Dr. Peebles hit me right between the eyes, too. He immediately told me of my subtle and "brilliant techniques" to remain invisible. Of course, he was right. I was a very, very shy child and that shyness has remained a part of my adult personality—and has often been misunderstood. He said that I came into this lifetime to work on visibility, to be more visible. He also talked of the rage I carried with me into this life. Some of that rage related to men—"those thick-headed, insensitive men," as Dr. Peebles put it. But he told me, ironically, it was my own male side that I trusted more than my female side. So my lesson in this life was to engage fully and embrace my femininity, which in itself has been somewhat difficult for me as I have had anger about it being a man's world, and for most of my earlier life had always felt in competition-or wanted to be in competition—with men. I was much a tomboy and often wished when I was young that I had been born a boy and maybe was a little pissed because I hadn't been. He also mentioned how I often carried the world on my shoulders—and I must say that burden has often weighed me down over the years. He also mentioned my deep sense of trance [mediumship] from this life and other lifetimes. I believe I was aware of most all this but I left there in denial and it would take several playings of the audio tape until I really *heard* what Dr. Peebles said to me. Don knew it, and he replayed the tape for me until I "got" it. In that moment of hearing, I was given an deep understanding of myself, probably for the first time ever. And I knew, without any doubt, that this spirit entity knew me better than I knew myself—and I could add—as well as Don knew me from the first moment our eyes had met across a crowded room.

So what had begun as a simple curiosity about mediumship developed into a study of Dr. Peebles and communication with the spirit world.

As a result of our encounter with the world of spirit, we wrote *To Dance With Angels: An Amazing Journey to the Heart with the Phenomenal Thomas Jacobson and the Grand Spirit, "Dr. Peebles,"* which was published in 1990. We *had* to share Dr. Peebles with the world. We could not keep this information to ourselves.

The new understandings of life and death and our continued research into near-death experiences (Don had two of his own NDE's), past life regression, spirit communication, miracles, and angel encounters, has been invaluable. Don and I both looked at life in a somewhat different way as a result. The magic and beauty that we both believed life held was intensified by our new discoveries. And I have to say that when Don died suddenly in October of 1995, I know my journey through grief has been much easier for me than it would have been had we not encountered the spirit world and the spiritual psychology of Dr. Peebles and his band of angels.

I have had ongoing contact with Don since his death. Some of it comes to me with the aid of Dr. Peebles as channeled through several mediums, some directly through my own automatic writing via pen and paper, through my clairaudient gift at the computer, or through messages relayed by various psychics.

Five months before his death, Don had written, "There is another reality enfolding ours—as close as our breath!"

Don was right. I know that without any doubt.

I thank Dr. Peebles, as I know Don does, for opening our hearts to the world of spirit.

I hope you enjoy and benefit from what you find within these pages. May you take the three principles of angelic wisdom into your heart and put them into action in your everyday life. If you do, I believe that you will be absolutely amazed at the results.

1

STRIKE UP THE BAND

○ ○

"If I know my own heart it beats in accord with the divine effort to better humanity, and throbs in tenderest love toward all races and the people of all lands."

—*James Martin Peebles, 1880*

On the night of March 23rd, 1922, a centennial birthday dinner was held in Los Angeles, California, for Dr. James Martin Peebles. The birthday celebration was one of warm companionship and camaraderie.

The banquet was hosted by Dr. Guy Bogart, a personal friend of Dr. Peebles and executive secretary of the Longer Life League. Hundreds were in attendance, including Bishop Cooper, Regionary Bishop of the Liberal Catholic Church; Methodist minister, the Reverend C. C. Pearce; Reverend Baker P. Lee, Rector Emeritus of Christ's Church; a former United States Senator, the honorable Cornelius Cole, himself ninety-nine years of age; a number of psychologists; members of the Independent Order of Good Templars; Theosophists; members of the Longer Life League; and members of the press.

To most in attendance that evening, one chair appeared to sit empty during dinner. That chair belonged to Dr. James Martin Peebles, the guest of honor.

Earlier that same afternoon, about a dozen of Dr. Peebles' close friends had gathered together to scatter the ashes of Dr. Peebles' terrestrial body in a rose garden of undisclosed location in compliance with Dr. Peebles' last wishes. Dr. Peebles had died on February 15th—only days short of his one hundredth birthday.

But for some who were attending the birthday celebration of their friend, the more than six-foot tall Doctor Peebles, with his warm, clear gray eyes, snowy white shoulder-length hair and long white beard, was present.

And for those who did not have highly developed psychic vision, Dr. Peebles' arrival was announced by Dr. Bogart just as dinner had ended.

Dr. Bogart explained that he had a message to relay from Dr. Peebles which would come from a "heavenly interview" conducted by a close friend of Dr. Peebles, former Chicago publisher and journalist, the late Herman Keuhn.

Through the agency of Dr. Bogart, acting as intermediary between earth and "Astraland," as he called the other side, Bogart had asked his spirit-guide, the dead journalist, Keuhn, if he would conduct an interview with the deceased Dr. Peebles. Keuhn had consented.

Dr. Bogart told those gathered that it was Dr. Peebles' wish that he sit in the latter's chair to transmit the message from the spirit world. Through the mediumship of Bogart, as relayed by heavenly reporter Keuhn, the message from Dr. Peebles came forward.

The guest of honor told his friends that there was no rheumatism in heaven—that his own rheumatism was a thing of the past. He told of the ineffable sweetness of heavenly melodies and the indescribable beauty of the colors in paradise. He also said that the "climate of Heaven resembles very much that of Southern California as it is pictured by the Chamber of Commerce."

Dr. Peebles reminded Dr. Bogart that he had spoken to Bogart, a couple of years previously, of how anxious he was to explore the moon and go journeying among the stars. Dr. Peebles announced that he was now getting his wishes granted.

He talked of how it all seemed "queer" to him over there, although he had nearly a lifetime of belief in the spirit world and a knowledge of its great laws. He said, "Man does not jump suddenly from one state of vibrations to another but carries into the astral, the mental and emotional vibrations which were strong in the last period in the flesh. You were aware of my long sickness before the passing across. When I awoke here I found myself sitting in a chair and warmly covered by blankets. Now, a spirit doesn't need blankets and warmth, but I had carried over enough of the earth vibrations to feel this need for a time."

Dr. Peebles went on to talk of mobility on the other side. "I am getting to be quite a floater. When a boy I used to look at pictures of angels with their wings. But we don't need wings here; we just move about at will. I had to have a nurse take me to my funeral, but I am mastering this locomotion in fine shape now."

An avid vegetarian for more than sixty years, Dr. Peebles stated that his friends should watch their diet and not neglect their exercises. He also stressed that one should keep an interest in life beyond the crematory, but to never let it diminish interest in the affairs of the physical world.

The extraordinary interview from the Spirit World was reported in the *Los Angeles Times,* the *New York Times*, the *Battle Creek Enquirer & News*, and other newspapers around the country.

The *New York Times* second front page story headlines read:

"SPIRIT SAYS HEAVEN HAS NO RHEUMATISM
Message From Dr. Peebles, Read at Post-Mortem Birthday Party, Tells of Bliss"

The *Los Angeles Times* second front page headline read:

"RHEUMATIZ IS MISSING IN HEAVEN
Dr. J. M. Peebles's Spirit Gives Joyous Message to Longer Life League"

In Battle Creek, Michigan, where Dr. Peebles had made his home for many years, the article was headed with:

"HEAVENLY INTERVIEW' FROM LATE DR. PEEBLES."

I suppose one could say that our press was much more open to spiritual matters during the early part of the twentieth century. It seems a little difficult to imagine that today's press would carry a headline story such as that in a serious vein.

It was always pretty much an acknowledged fact that seances were held in the White House during Abraham Lincoln's presidency, but in more recent time, during the Reagan administration, our modern day press ridiculed and laughed at Nancy Reagan when it was discovered that she had regularly consulted with an astrologer—something that many who had lived under the White House roof had done before her.

But beyond the openness of the press regarding spiritual or paranormal events in decades past, James Martin Peebles often made the pages of the *New York Times* throughout his incredible life. One might say he was a little out of the ordinary.

And he still is.

◆   ◆   ◆

The communication which came from the late Dr. Peebles at his postmortem birthday celebration was only the beginning of his on-going contact with those of us on this side of the veil. Throughout these more than seventy-five years since his death, Dr. Peebles has remained keenly interested in human destiny and has continued his spiritual work via the open channels of communication through the mediumship of various people all over the world.

A world renowned spiritualist of the nineteenth and early twentieth century, Dr. Peebles informs us that it is "his greatest joy and pleasure" to be able to communicate with us. His words, his personality, his wit and wisdom have been a great help to many over the years since he left his earthly existence. What I consider to be his "spiritual psychology," has given new understandings, guidance, and enlightenment to most who encounter his teachings.

Dr. Peebles tells us he is spokesman for a group of spirits and at the time he communicates from the spirit world he is surrounded by a band of angels, along with the spirit guides and deceased loved ones of those he is speaking to.

I became intrigued with the terrestrial Dr. Peebles more than ten years ago, shortly after encountering his spiritual wisdom, channeled through the trance-mediumship of Thomas Jacobson.

It was in the spring of 1987, when my late husband, author Don Pendleton and I, heard Dr. Peebles and Thomas on a popular syndicated Los Angeles KABC radio show, *Open Mind*, hosted by Bill Jenkins.

I had heard Bill Jenkins speak of Dr. Peebles prior to that Saturday night airing, but at the time it had not dawned on me that Bill Jenkins was speaking of a spirit entity.

What we heard that Saturday night on the talk radio show, left Don and I with a bit of awe. The insight Dr. Peebles gave callers was quite incredible. His words were filled with age-old wisdom, tinged with humor, and overflowing with love and compassion. The validity of his comments was apparent in the response from callers.

We were so intrigued that evening and decided we would have to experience Thomas Jacobson and Dr. Peebles for ourselves.

Don and I also decided, with our skepticism very much alive, that what was channeled by Thomas Jacobson was so profound and beautiful that the "source" of the beautiful personality of "Dr. Peebles" really did not matter—the messages he conveyed via Thomas Jacobson in a trance-state, were just too incredible and extraordinary for us to ignore.

Don had been a life-long metaphysical scholar and although he wrote fiction throughout most of his long writing career, his metaphysical ideas found their way into the pages of his books. He is considered to be the "father of the action/adventure genre" with his creation of

The Executioner series of novels, and his *Mack Bolan* character, which became a publishing phenomena following the release of his first book in the series of thirty-eight original novels, *War Against the Mafia*, in 1969. Action/adventure was a term he coined for marketing purposes. He considered the books to be a study in the metaphysics of violence and I'm sure it is the subtle nuances of metaphysics within those novels that has endeared those books to readers all over the world for many, many years.

I have had an interest in metaphysics and the paranormal for as long as I can remember. I was young when the story of Bridey Murphy hit the newspaper headlines all over the country. Ruth Simmons was a Colorado housewife who, while in a deep hypnotic trance, revealed a past life personality of Bridey Murphy, a woman who had lived in Ireland during the 1800's.

I was fascinated by the Bridey Murphy story. Morey Bernstein, the hypnotist, published his book, *The Search for Bridey Murphy*, in 1956.

I was also fascinated by the little I had heard about Edgar Cayce. Not long after, I read Thomas Sugrue's book on Cayce, *There is a River*.

Those two events intensified my interest in the paranormal, life after death, and reincarnation. I also had my own psychic gift from a young age. It would manifest in a "knowing" or at times, in precognition.

I had always thought it would have been so exciting to have encountered Edgar Cayce in person.

So when Don and I heard Dr. Peebles on the radio waves it was exhilarating to know that we may have encountered an experience very much like the late Edgar Cayce.

A short time later, we were to hear an audio tape of an *Open Mind* show from May, 1984, when Thomas and Dr. Peebles were guests. Another guest on that same show, via telephone hookup from Franklin, North Carolina, was George Meek, life-after-death researcher, author, and head of the Life Beyond Death Research Foundation. Two months prior to that show, George Meek had held a private session with Thomas and Dr. Peebles. He had found Dr. Peebles most impressive and commented that he had researched mediumship abilities in many countries over the previous fourteen years and that he had found Dr. Peebles to be one of the most knowledgeable and enlightened spirit persons with which he had talked.

Meek asked Dr. Peebles about a book written by J. M. Peebles, M.D., and originally published in 1869 and translated in several languages. The book, *Seers of the Ages: Embracing Spiritualism Past and Present*, was reissued for the last time in 1903 when Dr. Peebles was eighty-two years of age.

Dr. Peebles confirmed that he had, indeed, written the book, although he added that he could not take full credit for it as he had entered into trance states of automatic writing, of inspired writing, and ponderance in the meditational state. He considered it to be a collective effort. Meek asked Dr. Peebles if he would identify Aaron Knight to whom Dr. Peebles had dedicated the book.

Here is part of that dedication from the book:

> *Greeting to the Risen Spirit of Aaron Knight. Love is immortal. Golden is the chain that unites the past with the present. More beautiful is the spirit-blossom for the sweet love-budding of earth. Precious in spirit-history is Yorkshire, England—not so much for his noble descent and clerical culture, as for his happy home there, whose first memories of incarnate life, maternally pure, cling to his soul as lingering melodies from inspired minstrels. Passing early through the pale-curtained doorway of death, to his 'Pear Grove Cottage,' in the upper kingdoms of immortality, rapid and rhythmic has been thy march of progress...To me hast thou come in lone evening hours, bringing the dewy freshness of a foreshadowed morning, pearling the veiled moments of despair, diffusing inner sunshine and gladness; in wintry seasons of discontent, scattering delicious blooms, laden with love's incense, and speaking words of tenderness starry with promise—words so aglow with heavenly instruction as to make music in the blissful homes of the glorified...How indebted I am to thee for thy symbolic illustrations, logical acumen, originality of thought, and messages warm with sympathy from an overflowing heart!*

Spirit Brother! as a feeble token of appreciation and soul-felt grati-
tude, for thy watch-care and many favors, permit me to dedicate this
volume to thee, as one of my immortal Teachers.—J.M. Peebles, M.D.

On the radio show that night, Dr. Peebles confirmed for George Meek that he had dedicated the book to his spirit teacher, Aaron Knight. Dr. Peebles went on to explain, "Aaron was one who had facilitated my channel. Aaron was a medium [while on earth] who was never understood as a medium. He was almost taken off to the insane asylum a couple of times, for example. However, due to the influence of some of his friends—in Parliament, for example—he was not carted away. Due to my great joy with that state called craziness—I found a friend. He helped me to feel safe within myself. He helped me to create environments—using plants, using certain air waves, using coloration schemes—that greatly helped amplify the channeling."

I was to later discover in my research on the terrestrial Dr. Peebles that his spirit-guide Aaron Knight was born in Yorkshire, England, had died at the age of nineteen, and had been in the spirit world for more than two hundred and seventy years. He claimed to have ancestors of high repute and that his brother, the Reverend James Knight, was a distinguished clergyman of the English Church.

Aaron Knight was the main spokesman for the band of spirits who surrounded Dr. Peebles with love, and gave him guidance throughout his lifetime.

Don and I were to meet the grand spirit, Dr. Peebles in April of 1987, and that meeting filled us with awe, love and new understandings. It was an experience that had to be shared with others.

When we wrote our manuscript we knew only a little about who this spirit was when he lived on earth, but our curiosity and desire to know more launched us on a journey to learn as much as we could about James Martin Peebles. And there was much to learn!

◆   ◆   ◆

James Martin Peebles was born March 23, 1822, to James and Nancy Peebles at the homestead in Whitingham, Vermont. He was the oldest surviving child of a family of seven children—five sons and two daughters. From early childhood, James was magnetic, genial, benevolent, and witty. He was also known to be stubborn and capricious.

Peebles is a Scot name, traceable back to the seventh century. In the eleventh century the name was one of the most distinguished in the north of Europe. The ancestral family home is Peebleshire. More than three hundred years ago, a branch of the Peebles family left Scotland and settled in the north of Ireland. They were staunch Protestants with very pronounced religious convictions. They endured much persecution during a period of intense and bitter religious controversies. In 1718, they crossed the ocean and settled in Pelham, Massachusetts.

In the early 1800's, one of the descendants, James Peebles, left Massachusetts to settle in Whitingham, Vermont, near the Green Mountains. James was said to have been public spirited, zealous, patriotic and benevolent. He was a captain in the Vermont militia. In 1820, he married schoolmistress, Nancy Brown, who was of English descent. Nancy was the daughter of "Deacon Brown," a prominent citizen of Whitingham. The tall, good-looking, refined woman was said to have been endowed with intelligence, vivacity and wit. It was also said that her soul was free-born and she had a tendency to break through conservative restraints. Those characteristics would come to be bestowed on her first born son.

The young James was said to be restless. He had no interest in tasks and it was said that he hated grindstones, axes, churns and hoes. "We can never make any thing of James," was said more than once with a feeling of despair. The truth was they did not know the genius of the boy. He had a connection with nature, very much like his mother. He loved to tend the young lambs and would venture in the early morning springtime, with cold bare feet, over the snow mantled rocks and hollows to the pasture to see if any young lamb had been chilled by the night wind.

That wild Vermont countryside enchanted him. The flowers and birds were his companions, the maple poles his ponies, leaves and twigs his sailing vessels in the eddying pools. He gamboled with the minnows and tadpoles, and discovered all the cocoons, butterflies and robin's eggs. He sat on his native hills, watching everything his young eyes could take in, the stilly world at his feet.

He carried with him an undefinable feeling, a mystic consciousness, and a genius, as yet unfully expressed.

Years later, in poetic verse, he was to express,

> *While yet a boy I sought for ghosts, and sped*
> *Through many a listening chamber, cave, and ruin,*
> *And star-lit wood, the fearful steps pursing,*
> *High hopes of talk with the departed dead.*

When James Martin was twelve, the family pulled up stakes and moved to Smithville, New York. There James Martin attended a select school and excelled. At the age of sixteen, he, himself, was teaching school. Some of his students were older than he but James was gifted with tact and was soon on good terms with them all, enlisting a deep interest and enthusiasm in their studies. He entered the Oxford Academy to continue his studies while teaching high school. He studied Latin and Greek and the Classical Literature of the ancient periods. During that same time frame he was studying medicine under a well-known doctor, Oramel Martin.

Exposed to evangelical religion during this period, he soon was filled with skepticism and at times was disposed to regard all religion as a sham.

At about this time, Universalism began to attract public attention in Western New York. He attended a church meeting and was impressed and found it to be inspirational and moving and within a year became a convert to the "new faith." That became a turning point in his young life and at the age of twenty, he was ordained a Universalist minister. He preached his first sermon in McLean, New York. He was later to become pastor of the McLean church for five successive years following three years as pastor at Kelloggsville, New York. In 1844, he received his "Letter of Fellowship" and in 1846, he was ordained to the "work of an evangelist."

But his religious dogma was to soon expand. The young minister's opinions were in the formative stage and he was not yet sure how he should accept tradition as a finality, nor what limits he should impose in deciding the truth or falsity on theories predicated on scientific discoveries. Possessing an intimate love of the truth, he was also open and receptive to the inspirations of the new time that was dawning.

Spiritualism descended on America.

The young Reverend James reached out to it with wonder, joy and enthusiasm. The new light which began with the Shakers soon spread across the Western world. Millions were happy and filled with joy, for they had discovered the abiding places of their dearly departed.

Very much like what is happening again in today's world, people had reached a stage of thinking where the organized church no longer ministered to their spiritual needs. Many thinkers felt the church was full of hollow pretenses and they were becoming skeptical, tired of creeds, and many were drifting toward agnosticism.

But when Spiritualism dawned, the heavens suddenly became alive again! It electrified the spiritual silence, rekindled hope and faith, and returned mystical awareness to many.

The newspapers were filled with stories of spiritual events. Some were unbiased investigative accounts of spiritual occurrences. Others were reports of fraud and trickery.

But it was the traditional churches who expressed the most fear as they found their congregations moving away from tradition. The leaders of these institutions considered themselves to be guardians of those traditions and soon rallied forces and began to spread a dark cloud over the new light that had emerged.

But for many, they chose to stand in the new light and not let the shadow of darkness move over them.

Reverend James Martin Peebles was one who chose to stand in the bright light of Spiritualism.

And he did not stand alone. His band of angels were at his side.

It would not be long before he would become known as the "spiritual pilgrim."

Aaron Knight was the first of Rev. Peebles' "angels" to come to his attention. And throughout his lifetime he would commune with his spirit friends, not only within the silent moments of his mind, but through the mediumship of others.

His stand of free and independent thought would have some backlash for the young reverend and at times it was a struggle for him.

At one point, he had asked his spirit band if matters for him would be more promising.

Aaron Knight, as spokesman for the group of spirits, told James: "No, friend Peebles, your pathway is begirt with thorns, and jagged rocks will pierce your feet; your horoscope just before us is rough and stormy. We throw around your neck a chain of pearls, pearls which reflect your life, your plans, thoughts, purposes, deeds. All things are dual. These spiritually reflect your outer life, as your spiritual sensorium reflects your inner life. Symbolically, you are chained by these beautiful pearls. A lady friend of yours, clad in robes of purity, known among us as 'Queen of Morn,' and in your world as 'Madame Elizabeth,' sister of Louis XVI of France, from this chain, which I put around your neck, has suspended a cross, indicative of trials and crucifixions in your pilgrimage. But be of good cheer, you shall overcome, and every sorrow will give fragrance to the bud that blossoms over your heart."

Not many months after, Madame d'Obeney, a celebrated traveler and Spiritualist, met James in the East and surprised him with a gift, significant of the pearls mentioned by the spirits, consisting of a string of beads carved from the wood of an olive tree that grew on Mt. Olivet, in the very garden of Gethsemane, where Jesus prayed that the bitter cup might pass from him.

James then had a cross made after the pattern shown by the spirits—the front of it of beautiful pearl—the pearl of wisdom, the back of gold—the gold of love, on which was engraved the names of the nine spirits in his band of angels: Lorenzo Peebles, his brother who had died as a child; Aaron Knight, the Elucidator; Mozart, the Spiritual Harmonizer; Madame Elizabeth, the Love-angel; Parasee Lendanta, an Italian scientist; Hosea Ballou, known as the Sermonizer; Caná, known as the Positivist; James Leonard; John W. Leonard, a clergyman from Edinburgh, Scotland.

Some time later Dr. Peebles was to encounter a spirit-artist who painted a likeness of his spirit guide, Madame Elizabeth. The artist painted her wearing a gemmed crown upon her beautiful brow, and to his surprise, wearing a chain similar to his, around her neck.

Not long after, he was walking the streets of Boston when he felt as if he was suddenly directed into an antiquarian library. He browsed some and was about to turn to leave the store when he was drawn instinctively to the "French" section. As if a magnetic shock came over him, he stooped down and put his hand on a history of Louis XVI, and therein found a likeness of the King and his sister Elizabeth, resembling that of her in the spirit painting—hair the same, and a chain of pearls around her neck, with a cross attached.

This left Dr. Peebles with a strengthened faith in his guides and made him buoyant in spirit. He became more conscious of angel-presence around him, he came to soon understand that his band of angels was larger than the nine aforementioned. There were two intertwining bands associated with Dr. Peebles: Powhattan, known as the Magnetic Cleanser; a Pawnee Chief; two doctors known as the Analyzers; a quaint and witty Irishman;—and John, the Beloved, around whom the whole band revolves as planets around their central sun.

James Martin Peebles joined his spirit band on February 15th, 1922, and the mystical melodies that they render from their home within the heavens echo across space and time—piercing the thin, misty veil which serves as an illusion of separation. We, and they, are of one world—and *all* of us *are spiritual beings*.

Dr. Peebles, the spiritual pilgrim, has taken on a new role since he shed his physical body and left it behind. He is now spokesman for his spirit band of angels and to his earthly titles of Clergyman, Doctor of Medicine, Doctor of Philosophy, and Author, has been added what may be his highest degree yet—Doctor of Spiritual Psychology.

2

THE SPIRITUAL PILGRIM

o o o o o o o o o o o o o o o o o o o o o o o o o o o o o o

"Life is a pilgrimage; let us kindly help each other along the tiresome journey; for soon, perhaps, shall we put our sandals off, and lay our weary burdens down by the cypress-trees that shade Death's peaceful river. And when that tremulous hour comes, as it must to each and all, precious will be the memories of kind words spoken, and the good that we have done."

—*James Martin Peebles, 1880*

The spiritual psychology that Dr. Peebles shares with us is an outgrowth of his own earthly consciousness, but now, from his new perspective, his spiritual understandings are fuller and broader regarding the purpose of our earthly lives.

One remarkable difference in his understanding revolves around reincarnation. While on earth he did not believe in reincarnation as such. He did believe in the pre-existence of the soul, and as a Spiritualist, he held very closely to the tenets of Spiritualism. He believed in immortality and that consciousness lived on, and that each of us had to answer for our behavior, especially if it strayed from a Christ-like love. He believed in God as the Infinite Spirit Presence of the Universe, to live one's life in a true, noble and Christ-like way and to hold conscious communion with spirits and angels.

Dr. Peebles once wrote, "It is my prayer—the soul-aim of my life, to live and walk in the spirit of Christ."

15

He devoted his life to his love of God and his fellow man. He savored the beauty of nature—spending the dawn of each morning communing with his flowers and fruit trees and listening to the songbirds welcoming the new day. His scholarly mind soaked up classical literature, the works of poets, and the philosophies of great minds throughout history. He spread the word of God and of his angels at every opportunity and on every podium which welcomed him. He sailed the seas, and stepped onto foreign lands with a message of love. He prolifically penned his thoughts in books and newspapers all over the world. He integrated his medical knowledge with his psychic knowing to heal the sick, and often without the sick being physically in his presence. He spoke out with authority and fervor against man's inhumanity to man. He lived a full life in those ninety-nine years—a life filled with love, inspiration, adventure and exploration.

Dr. Peebles authored more than thirty books, many pamphlets, and endless magazine and newspaper articles, throughout his life, most centered around his spiritual beliefs or his spiritual journeys. Most were published in several editions and in a number of foreign language editions.

One of his books, *Vaccination, A Curse and a Menace to Personal Liberty*, can be found today in several University medical libraries. The book speaks to his outrage of the dangers, criminality and political influences of arm to arm smallpox vaccination—a controversial subject at the end of the nineteenth century. It was originally published in 1900 and several editions followed.

At the age of forty-three, James Martin Peebles completed his medical studies at the University of Medicine and Surgery at Philadelphia and received his medical degree. The completion of his medical studies followed his Civil War service, where in 1863—1864, he served in a clerical and medical capacity under Captain Damon Kilgore and Grant and Howard's army in Tennessee and Alabama. It has been said that he refused a Chaplain's officer commission as he held strong to his pacifist views.

In July of 1870, President Ulysses S. Grant appointed Dr. Peebles to serve as U. S. Consul to Trebisond, Turkey. It seems to be unclear how the appointment came about except for two things. Damon Kilgore, who he had served under in the war, was a well-known Philadelphia attorney and may have had some political influence, and Dr. Peebles was serving on the Congressional Indian Peace Commission which had consisted of Generals Harney, Sheridan, Sherman, Sanborn, and others.

◆   ◆   ◆

The indigenous peoples of America had always held a special place in Dr. Peebles' heart. After becoming aware that some of his spirit guides were American Indian, he felt an even closer bond to the trials and tribulations of the Indian tribes which had for centuries graced our homeland—their homeland.

Around 1860, when Dr. Peebles had been in California on one of his spiritual pilgrimages, he was taking one of his evening walks for meditation and interior communion. That evening, he ascended a terrace in the foothills of the Sierra Nevada.

The scene before him was magnificent as the wide stretches of the San Joaquin Valley presented one splendid panorama, while a soft blue haze settled on the summits of the coastal range some seventy miles away. He found the scene inspiring and felt about him a vast concourse of spirits—spirits of the Indians who had once occupied the area. He addressed the spirits and his voice resonated through the rocky caverns, and his tones were caught by some passing miners who stopped to listen to the strange discourse. As the miners returned to their camp, word spread quickly that some crazy man was on the mountain talking to a ghost!

If only those miners had known. There were many ghosts who walked the same paths, side by side with them, in those Sierra foothills.

Another time, in Wisconsin, Dr. Peebles had communed with the Indian spirits at that locale. At the lakeshore home of J. O. Barrett, Dr. Peebles and other guests were standing before a wigwam that Mr. Barrett had built on his forested property and about to begin a spiritual meeting when Dr. Peebles turned to face the moonlit lake. He addressed the Indian spirits, reminding them of their sufferings, of the injustice meted out to them for centuries, of the bloody resolution of the whites to exterminate their brethren in the West, and of his determination to defend their rights by the establishment of systems of peace.

Sometime later, during a seance, an Indian spirit cordially thanked the "Pale-face" for his "big talk in the wigwam."

At another time, Dr. Peebles asked Powhatten, who was being channeled by the medium, Dr. Dunn, about his earth and spirit home. In poor English, Powhatten replied, "Me had, when in my body, one squaw. Some Indians have many. Me had one pappose, *Kanawaubish,* 'Pretty Water;' You call my pappose 'Pocahontas.' Me still be Indian; me no speak good like white man; me got nice wigwam home by big waters. Me got pretty canoe, and bow and arrow; me hunt, but no kill; me sleep under blue sky; me have for me bed the big spirit hunting grounds. Me blanket be the great blue heaven. Me music is the waving trees and the breath of the Big Spirit, as he blows leaves of the forest. In morning time, the Great Spirit looks out from his window in the east, and the Indian, with dew on his forehead, worships the Great Spirit in the sun. Me now like the white man, and me come with many chiefs, of many tribes, to do him good."

Dr. Peebles' whole soul was stirred to intense action in defense of the Indians. He was determined to put a stop to the extermination. Here is a letter he wrote in 1868 to his friend and colleague, A. H. Love, who was president of the Universal Peace Society, of which Dr. Peebles had once been vice-president:

"Passing down the main street of Leavenworth, I saw a recruiting office; and reaching Topeka, on board the train for Lawrence were four cars loaded with cavalry officers. I saw the whitened tents of the soldiery. The army was awaiting orders to march upon the Indians. Oh, how my heart ached and my soul bled! Constituting myself a peace commissioner, I immediately called upon Gov. Crawford and the State Marshall, and protested, in kindness yet in *great firmness*, against this proposed movement to be conducted by Gen. Sheridan. I went on still west from Topeka, toward Colorado, conversing with Judge Humphrey, Col. Smith, and other army officers. It seemed as though God's angels aided me in thought and speech. These officers admitted the wisdom and beauty of my humanitarian position; but they were 'Utopian and *impracticable*,' they said; 'and adapted to times a hundred years hence.'

"Perhaps I am too enthusiastic for the red man, our brother, God's child. Perhaps I am too enthusiastic for peace throughout the world. But my soul's sympathies are stirred; and now, while I pen these lines, my eyes are suffused with tears.

"I am sorely tried. The Commissioners, save Col. S. F. Tappen, seem inclined to take retrograde steps. It is impossible to get to the Indians now personally: they suspect everybody. If there could be a *delegation* gotten up in some way, in connection with the 'Peace Commissioners,' having the sanction of Government, I think something might be done; but between now and spring, how many will be shot down by a barbarous soldiery! I sometimes feel like flying away from the Christian civilization, so false to justice and benevolence, and going off alone into the Indian country, devoting my life to their good."

The following winter, the Congressional Indian Peace Commission invited Dr. Peebles, as a volunteer, to visit the Indians who were then fighting with the Whites in the Sioux and Rocky Mountain regions, for the purpose of organizing treaties, to end the blood shed, and to befriend the Indians, allowing them their natural rights to live on the American continent.

Dr. Peebles gathered testimony from various senators and generals who agreed that the actions against the Indians were disgraceful; he gathered quotes from the speeches of Indian chiefs who were asking for justice; he talked with W. P. Ross, chief of Cherokees and with other educated Indians who demonstrated their capacity to be civilized. With burning words, Dr. Peebles published editorials in *The Banner of Light*, a leading worldwide Spiritualist newspaper.

One of his editorials in *The Banner of Light* found its way into newspapers all across the country. This is what he wrote:

"Our Saxon face is mantled with shame, and soul humbled in deepest humiliation, at the individual and associate crimes that blot the escutcheon of the great, wicked Christian country, called the United States of America. Crimes red as blood, vindictive as death, and black as the cinders of Pluto's pit; crimes willful, determined, and continuous too, against the Indian tribes of the West, Northwest, and Southwest! Is justice, is philanthropy, dead? Is progress a dream? and sympathy a mere historic legend? Our heart aches; our tears flow. God, angels, American citizens of better thought and life, tell us what we can, what we *ought,* to do to check this nation from further cheating, swindling, sacking, shooting, slaughtering, and murdering, through its officers, superintendents, and agents, the three hundred thousand remaining aborigines of this country? A government is responsible for the agents it employs and pays. In this country the people, with ballot in hand, are the government: accordingly *you,* readers, directly or indirectly, are possible for the defrauding and murdering of those red men west of the Mississippi.

"Our government must give those three hundred thousand Indians the protection of law; must give them a civil-rights bill; must treat them as men; must grant them their annuities, and guard them against thieving agents, trafficking vagabonds, and a murderous soldiery; for they are God's children, and our brothers. This course pursued, and a continuous *peace* is secured with our red brothers of the West,—brothers originally noble in nature, firm in their friendships, and keen in their perceptions of the principles of natural justice.

"Though treated as they have been by the whites, those that tread the shadow-lands of eternity are returning good for evil by descending from their hunting-ground homes in the heavens, with balms of healing, and words of love and cheer. Hours, days, months, in the past, have we talked with Powhattan, through the organism of a medium friend, relative to the past, present, and future of the Indians upon this continent. 'Tis only justice to say, we have ever found this chief the very soul of simplicity, tenderness, truthfulness, and a genuine magnanimity. Blessings be upon Powhatten, Red Jacket, Tecumseh, Black Hawk, Thunder, Logan, Little Crow, Osceola, Antelope, and all Indian spirits that are shedding their healing magnetisms and peace-influences upon the inhabitants of earth."

It would be some time for peace to truly come but Dr. Peebles moved ahead in a passionate fight for justice and peace. He had carried this same passion into his active fight for abolition of slavery, where he stood on the lecture platform beside William Lloyd Garrison, Garret Smith, Henry White, Sojourner Truth and others, and with his stand for Woman's Suffrage and any other cause for individual freedom and justice. He served on the International Peace Commission and represented the U.S. Arbitration League at the 1886 conference in Berlin. He was, indeed, a true humanitarian.

◆   ◆   ◆

When I set out to research Dr. Peebles' terrestrial life I had no idea what an adventure it would be. It took a lot of heavy research but during the process I was to discover that at times things would just "fall into my hands." More than once, I had made phone calls and they turned out to be a dead-ends or so I had thought. People were very generous in their information and their comments led me off in another direction which would turn out to be where I needed to be. The synchronicity was quite something at times. Quite by "accident" I came across a researcher that was able to uncover a mountain of information for me, not only in the Battle Creek, Michigan area where Dr. Peebles had made his home for many years, but all kinds of valuable information related to his life. I soon came to believe that Dr. Peebles and his angels were directing me.

One time I had asked a small used book store to do a book search for me to find any of Dr. Peebles' rare books. I had periodically checked with the store but they failed to turn up any books. Several months went by, about nine, and I was driving home from an appointment and something told me to stop at that store which was a few blocks from my home. I was running late and had told Don I would be home long before, so I argued with myself (or whoever was giving me that message to go to that store). As I drove closer to home and the store, I continued to get that message and I continued to argue that I didn't have time and I did not want to worry Don. Well, almost as if guided by something beyond me, my car pulled into the left turn lane and pulled into the small shopping center and parked in front of the store. As I went in, I wondered why I was moved to be there. I looked around the shelves for any of Don's out of print books, thinking that was the reason to be there. I was about to leave the store without speaking to the owner as she was busy with another customer when the customer turned and walked out the door just as I moved toward the counter. I stopped at the counter and asked the owner if she had ever had any response to a book search she had done for me some months earlier. She asked what I was looking for and I gave her Dr. Peebles' name. To my surprise, she pulled out a card from her file and said, "Oh, yeah. I found a book of his but it was so expensive I didn't think you'd want it. Here's the name of the guy that had it, if you're interested." I couldn't grab it out of her hand fast enough. Did I want it?!! I couldn't believe this woman. She had heard about this book nearly seven months before and had not bothered to call me! I immediately telephoned the man. He lived in upstate New York and was a collector of Shaker materials. He still had the book in his collection and it was on the way to me the next day. It definitely helps to listen to your angels!

Not only did my research journey take me all over this country but it also took me to Australia, London, India and elsewhere. Dr. Peebles had been a busy man. He lived in many places around the United States and he had traveled the world five times. His first trip had been in 1865 aboard the Cunarder Persia, an iron paddle wheel steamship. His return of his fifth trip around the world was reported by the *New York Times* in June of 1913 as he arrived in New York aboard the Atlantic Transport liner, Minnehaha, sailing from London. He was ninety-one. At that time it was reported that he planned to take his next trip in the fall of 1915. He wrote of those trips in his books, *Around the World,* first published in 1875, and in *Three Journeys Around the World* and the last edition, *Five Journeys Around the World.*

Dr. Peebles was married to Mary Conkey, a teacher, in 1852. Their union produced three babies who died apparently through miscarriage or at birth. They adopted a young boy, Louie, who died at the age of ten while Dr. Peebles was on the preaching trail in California. The child's death was most difficult for him, as it was for his wife.

It appeared that the marriage may have been only one of convenience as their lives were not attuned to the same universal harmonies. Mary was said to be a very intelligent woman, an artist, but her life focused on domestic ties, neatness and order. She was strictly observant of social proprieties, reserved and cautious in her friendships. Dr. Peebles, on the other hand, did not focus at all on the domestic, but on his literary work, and he belonged exclusively to the public. He had little time for domestic chit-chat or companionship and was said to be rather undemonstrative and impersonal and his love for people seemed to be more universal in nature rather than intimate. It is said that many women were drawn to his charismatic personality but would soon become disillusioned and disappointed that he did not fall in love with them nor was interested in pursuing their affection. Although it seems that Mary did not travel with her husband, or spend much time with him, the marriage remained intact despite the fact that they often lived apart throughout the years. Mary either lived at their home in Battle Creek or later in Hammonton, New Jersey, while Dr. Peebles was living in Cincinnati, San Antonio, San Diego or elsewhere, and spending long periods of time on the lecture circuit. Mary died at their home in Hammonton, New Jersey, in 1909 at the age of eighty-three. Her obituary did not indicate if her husband was with her at the time of her sudden death.

Don and I had the opportunity to spend some time with an elderly man who had known Dr. Peebles in the flesh. We had been attempting to locate this man since the time he had attended one of Thomas Jacobson's appearances at a church in Los Angeles. The man had reported to Thomas that he had once attended a lecture by this Dr. Peebles in Los Angeles. And after hearing Dr. Peebles through the mediumship of Thomas, his comment was, "he hasn't changed a bit."

In the summer of 1990, we met with and interviewed Nelson Westphalen at his home in West Los Angeles. Nelson was charming and humorous. He had celebrated his ninetieth birthday the previous December. "As a young man," Nelson recalled, "I had the privilege of attending a meeting in Los Angeles when Dr. Peebles was a guest speaker for George Francis, popular psychic of the time. It was on the 8th floor of the old Hamburger Building at 8th at Broadway in downtown Los Angeles. I'll never forget that night, and I have held both George Francis and Dr. Peebles close to my heart ever since."

Nelson's wife, Dorothy, confirmed for us, that indeed, Nelson had often spoke of the impact that Dr. Peebles and George Francis had on him when he was a young man.

Nelson told us that when he heard that Thomas Jacobson would be channeling Dr. Peebles at the Church of the Inner Light in 1987, he could hardly wait to hear Dr. Peebles to see if it was the man he had known in about 1920.

Nelson shared with us his meeting with the spirit of Dr. Peebles. "Well, so I was very interested in hearing Thomas Jacobson and seeing if this was real [the channeling]. But I knew it was him [Dr. Peebles] the minute he started speaking. Same powerful voice, same Scottish accent, the same humor and the same wisdom. I had a chance to ask a question, so I decided to ask about George Francis, who also of course has been dead for many years.

"Dr. Peebles replied that he still saw George on the spirit side from time to time, and that his favorite topic for conversation was still 'man's inhumanity to man.' That sealed it right there. I had to slap my leg. That was George's favorite theme while I knew him."

Nelson described Dr. Peebles as a dynamic man even at a time when he was coming up on one hundred years. He remembered that Dr. Peebles stood tall, used a cane, and was accompanied by an attractive, full bosomed, younger woman. That cane may have been the one that Dr. Peebles was given by the wife of his friend, Dr. Sayre and which Dr. Peebles bequeathed to Dr. Sayre in his will.

Thomas did a trance session for Nelson that afternoon and Nelson was thrilled to again speak with Dr. Peebles. We gave Nelson and Dorothy an autographed copy of our book. We saw Nelson one more time, and sadly, he died several months later.

The following summer, Don and I were invited to the wedding of the son of dear friends. It was to be in Port Orchard, near Seattle, Washington, quite some distance from our home in Southern California. Don and I decided to go. So we headed northward by car. Before leaving, Thomas Jacobson had told us to be sure and visit Port Townsend while we were in Washington as it was a pretty town. Following the wedding, we decided to drive up to Port Angeles to take the ferry across to Victoria, British Columbia. On the way, we drove the few miles out of our way to Port Townsend. Port Townsend sits out on the tip of the Olympic Peninsula at the entrance to Puget Sound, a seaside community of seven thousand people, noted for its numerous examples of Victorian architecture—a charming little town.

In exploring the town we went into two bookstores (we've always had a weakness for bookstores) and then couldn't resist going into a used/rare bookstore. I'm always looking for rare copies of Dr. Peebles' books and writings on Spiritualism of the nineteenth and early twentieth century. I found two old books to buy—neither connected to Dr. Peebles. While asking the sales clerk if he remembered having any books by James Martin Peebles, a lovely young woman interrupted me to exclaim, "My grandfather knew Dr. Peebles."

My immediate, excited response was, "He did! Where?"

To which she replied, "Los Angeles." She went on to tell me that a recent book had been written about Dr. Peebles and that....

With a big smile I interrupted to inform her, "I know; I'm Linda Pendleton."

It was her turn to fall over! She was the granddaughter of Dorothy Westphalen who had married Nelson Westphalen quite late in life.

The granddaughter mentioned that Nelson's and Dorothy's autographed copy of our book had been on her bedside nightstand in Los Angeles and she had been reading it prior to leaving for her vacation in Washington.

The serendipitous question we asked—who was responsible for the chance encounter at the tip of the Olympic Peninsula some 1200 miles from Los Angeles?—was it Nelson or another favorite soul who set that up for us? Or could it have been a collaboration between two "old friends" on the spirit side, who both possess an incredible sense of humor?

I believe we could "hear" both Dr. Peebles and Nelson laughing.

All in all, it seems to be confirmation that we are members of a large spirit "family"—and they never let us forget it. This is an incredibly small world, after all.

And the angels are always at our side.

3

ILLUSIONS OF SEPARATION

o o o o o o o o o o o o o o o o o o o o o o o o o o o o o o

"The greatest illusion is that you are alone; never are you alone."

—*The grand spirit, Dr. Peebles*

The wisdom and spiritual psychology of Dr. Peebles can bring tremendous understanding and insight to our lives. His words may not hold all the magical answers that we may be looking for, but his words can encourage us to appreciate the magic of life, the beauty within each soul, including our own, and to look at life, and death, with new understanding. His words, and the words of others on the spirit side, can bring comfort and a deep sense of peace as we struggle with our life experiences. For many, the teachings of the grand spirit, Dr. Peebles, has had a life-changing effect on their lives. His wisdom carries with it the essence of truth which hits us at a heart/soul level. It may be the same truths we have heard or read before, but for some reason had chosen to deny or ignore, not fully taking it into our consciousness.

Dr. Peebles' spiritual psychology is not enigmatic or esoteric. It is a simple and basic truth which can be easily incorporated into one's life. But at times it can be profound and very significant to our own personal journey of spiritual understanding. His teachings can be used in our everyday lives with ease and success. He is a great teacher, and although he probably would not take full credit for his teachings from the spirit world, much in the same way as he would not take full credit for some of his writings while on earth, whatever wisdom is incorporated into his words comes from a higher understanding and is filled with love and compassion.

Dr. Peebles' teachings have, for many, been inspirational and life-changing. It is now time for Dr. Peebles to speak again, and this time, he speaks through me. My own psychic gift has expanded in recent years and my clairaudience has enhanced. When Dr. Peebles had told me more than ten years ago that I would one day be channeling him and others, I laughed. The idea of surrendering to trance-channeling did not appeal to me at all. I did not even consider at the time that the mode of mediumship might be different. I did know, though, that if Don passed to the other side before me that he would be in contact with me. I was right about that. He has been, from within hours after his sudden death, in many ways, some subtle and some not so subtle. He continues to work with me on my writing—both from an inspirational mode and from a conscious mode. And I love it! He has also been in contact with me through several people who professionally channel Dr. Peebles, and through other psychics.

So now, we will commune with the angels.

◆   ◆   ◆

Linda: Dr. Peebles, I would like for you to share with us your insight on our conscious state of separation.

Dr. Peebles: God bless, you, Linda. We are delighted to again be working with you. As you know, your loving soulmate, Don, is by my side and he, too, will be having some input into the things we share with you for your book.

Linda: Yes, I know he is, Dr. Peebles. When he is not by your side, he is by mine. I love you both.

Dr. Peebles: Well, yes, yes he is. He says, "Never far away my love, my beautiful Linda." And we all love you. Now, you ask about separation. And you are right. For most, it becomes a conscious separation. Each of you have come to Earth for a specific reason. It is there on Earth, a classroom of learning, that you study the *illusions of separation*. Separation from God, separation from others, separation from all of life and separation from your very own soul. The lessons are not easy on the Earth school and many find it difficult to break through the illusion which exists in the mind and to discover that it is just that—an illusion.

Is it not a paradox that in order to understand the unconditional love which God has for each soul, that unconditional love has to begin within yourself? Are you not often last on the list? Don't you often ask, "How can God love me?" When you come to the place of understanding that God is non-judgmental, is loving without restriction or condition, then is the time in which you can look at yourself in the same bright light. And in doing so, it enables you to not only forgive yourself for what one might consider to be weakness or failure, but to love who you are. And always remember you are a spiritual being—caught up in the physical body—but connected to the God source, the God energy, and to every other creature that walks the Earth. That includes not only your family, your lover, your neighbor, your countryman, but every life form which exists on the planet.

But you say, how can I love me?—me, who is not perfect like God?—me, who is not as good as I could be?—me, who is a failure at life?—me, who is unloving?—and the list goes on and on. As you struggle to know yourself, you often fail to look at who you really are. Again a reminder. You are a spiritual being who comes from the creation of God. You are in His image. You are mighty and powerful, you are of the essence of God and within that essence is love. Love, L-O-V-E.

Within the illusions that surround one, is fear. Let me say to you, that never are you alone. I know that at times it may feel that way. I, myself, often experienced that in my Earth life. I would feel the pressures of every day existence, of not having the respect I so desired, and at times would experience the aloneness of a silence which echoed through the dark night. But then I would remember my spirit band of angels. All I had to do was to call on them. They were always there, seldom intrusive, but there in quiet waiting for me to call out to them. But I also, like many of you, had times of doubt, need of validity, and although I had a never-ending and unfaltering love for mankind, I often pulled into myself, turning away from expressions of love and what one could call intimacy. Not on a sexual level, but on a soul-level. I endured the illusion of separation, yet, I cried out at times to God and the spirit world for understanding and connection. Each time I did, my prayer was answered. I was given comfort in the dark places of my mind and heart.

So I say to you, never are you alone, even in the darkest moments of despair or fear. And never are you unloved, nor can you escape love, for love is the essence of all things.

Each of you have guides and angels around you. They have been with you since you journeyed from this dimension into that one. They are your friends, your supporters, your teachers. They are there to help you through the bad times and the good. They are there to comfort you in times of distress, or pain. They are there to give you guidance. They are there to help you to shed the illusion of separation which you carried with you into life. They are there to help you remember who you are. And they are there to bless you with God's love.

Linda: Dr. Peebles, why did we come here with this illusion of separation?

Dr. Peebles: It is a study of love. Those of you who chose to come to Earth for earthly experiences, came to strive toward a higher understanding. It is one of the many levels of higher learning. Think of Earth as a schoolroom. Within that class, you learn the scheduled curriculum and at the end of that school year you graduate, so to speak, and it is time to advance to a higher grade. There are many schools to attend to study different areas of learning. Many souls are on this side of the veil, but many are at other Earth-like places. It is a free choice where one might take classes, although some of the higher teachers may suggest you might want to attend one particular school or university to obtain the best education.

Some of us have chosen to teach from here. But that also is part of our own personal growth. For me, I love what I do. It is fulfilling, joyous and my greatest pleasure. And I, too, am a student. I learn not only from those I communicate with, but from those in the spirit world who share their insight and guidance with me. It is not a one way street. All of us, here or there, gain from these experiences.

In order to understand that you carry with you only an *illusion* of separation, to reach that spiritual truth, you have to first allow yourself to love God and then to love yourself. Only then, when you are comfortable with the truth of that love, can you then reach out to life around you.

Earth is also a school of relationships, with yourself, with others and with all of life. But in order to understand those relationships you must understand that separation does not exist. It is only an illusion of the mind.

Now regarding the illusion of separation while in the physical body, if you already knew all the answers why would you take the course? Of course, you do at your soul level know the answers, but in order to have a greater experience, a greater challenge, a greater understanding, some sort of obstacle has to be overcome. For all of us, in the spirit world or on Earth, our graduation into enlightenment and the true God energy only comes from experience. And to reach that place of unconditional love and divine truth can take many lifetimes of experience. Eternity is not a stagnate or static place, it is a place of continued and evolving growth. And at some point in the evolution of time, as you know time, one may reach the ultimate God source. But in the meantime, spiritual life is full of exciting experiences, knowledge beyond comprehension, and love and understanding beyond your wildest dreams and imaginations.

The illusions of separation for many can be a challenge—a life-long process to achieve illumination—but it can also be an instantaneous illumination when it is understood that there is no separation. The little child in his innocence still has ties to the spiritual world. Is it not a shame that the fears and bias of the adult do not allow the child to hold on to their spiritual understanding? Instead, the innocence is taken away and fears are inherited—the thinking of the child is clouded, and memory of the spirit world becomes dim, as his young mind filters in fear and uncertainty. But that too, is part of the studies of the Earth-school. The challenge then, is to come back to that place of spiritual understanding—to remember once again that there is no separation from the divine—to renew the child-like innocence.

Linda: While you are on the subject of the innocence of children, I seem to sense that the children who are now coming into the world are coming forth with a spiritual awareness that seems different or more advanced than past generations. Is something like that happening?

Dr. Peebles: Yes. You, Linda, like many others, are very observant. There has been a shift in recent time as civilization is returning to a balance, uh, a swinging of the pendulum, so to speak, where a sense of brotherhood, an understanding of soul connection becomes prominent in the mind and hearts of many. These children come with a higher spiritual awareness and even an intellectual advancement which readies them for the technological age which is really just in its infancy. You see the spark in their eyes, the expansion of awareness of life, and a spiritual awareness which may not be blocked out or taken from them quite as easily as in the past. The shift which is taking place as the new millennium approaches will gradually move mankind to a new level of spiritual understanding, and might I say, long overdue. But change does not take place in the blink of an eye—from your perspective—but it is in motion and, an accelerated motion. Many of you already feel the acceleration and many will see the results. It is in the eyes of these children who have chosen to come at this time—they bring with them a spiritual excitement, and do not expect them to stand still and be silent. Their energy will spread like wild-fire.

When one comes to understand that everyone is a part of God, then a sense of oneness prevails and infiltrates all areas of life. As you look out to the blue sky above—to the sun glistening across the sea; to the trees and flowers which sprout up from the rich soil of Mother Earth; to the creatures who fly in the skies, walk upon the land, and swim in the waters;—as you look out to your neighbor, allowing the differences which may be there and appreciating the diversity, whether it be color or race, cultural or social, philosophical or religious; to those who may be less fortunate than you; to the criminal who walks the street and forces himself upon you; to the sick and crippled; to those in emotional pain; to each and every one of your community, your state, your nation and stretch beyond that to encompass everyone who is on your planet—each and every one of God's creatures,—only then, when you can see the God essence which is within all, when your eyes can look with unconditional love, when your heart sings God's love, can you truly understand and accept that there is no separation—*All* is of God. And then peace comes to your soul. And the angels and God rejoice.

Now, let's talk again about fear. It is human nature to desire safety and sanctuary. The instinct for survival does not belong only to humans, it is a part of nature, too. But the fear of not having security—safety, can disable one on their journey if too much emphasis is placed upon it. Yes, it is natural to want to be safe from harm, to find sanctuary away from the tribulations of life, but often in struggling to ensure those desires, one may pull away, retreat from life and in doing so, the illusion of separation again rears its head. Fear can make one's life stagnate, unproductive, lonely, and painful. If one can welcome those fears, face them head-on and embrace them, then they will disintegrate like the ashes of a burning log. Now fire can bring fear—a hot flame that is licking up the walls of your home—but from a different perspective, flames generated under an oak log can fill the room with warmth and comfort, and when either fire burns out, and you pick up the cool ashes which remain and let them sift through your fingers, they disintegrate as they fall to earth. So it is perspective. *Do I fear because I do not have food in my cupboards?—or a roof over my head?—or do I fear because I do not have stacks of food in my cupboard or the roof of a mansion over my head?* Do you see the paradox?

So it is my suggestion that fear be looked at, embraced, and then released. To hang on to it, only causes pain. Then we have to embrace pain in order to let go of it. It can be a cycle of desperation and unhappiness. So let the fear go before it engulfs you.

You see, those are the lessons of the illusions of separation. The lessons revolve around love, fear, pain. In learning the lesson of separation, you learn the greatest lesson of unconditional love, with God, with yourself and with others. You learn that fear has no basis, because you are a spiritual being—and never are you alone—and it is up to you how you react and perceive. And pain is also there to teach you a lesson, and when you can learn to embrace both fear and pain, they will dissolve just like the handful of ashes. Do you understand?

Linda: Yes, I do. But I can sure see to learn these lessons can be difficult, can't it?

Dr. Peebles: Yes, it can be. But remember, that is your purpose for attending the Earth-school. Those are the challenges presented in the Earth-curriculum, and is the only way spiritual growth is accomplished. So, enjoy the lessons, savor them, and know that those lessons are part of a greater purpose. To reach a higher level of spiritual evolution within the classroom is coming to pass. But it begins within each of you and then it grows, like a snow ball gathering snow as it rolls down a hill. When it reaches the bottom of the hill and comes to rest, it will be much larger, much greater than when it started its descent. It is the same for your soul. As it gathers experiences and expands, it becomes much larger, much greater. And that new form retains its shape forevermore.

Linda: Dr. Peebles, what can you say to someone who may be overwhelmed by their fears, may be feeling the deep pain of grief or feeling completely hopeless and that there is no way out of their pain? And what can we do to help someone like that through their pain, to help them see that joy and peace may return to their life, that everything can get better?

Dr. Peebles: As I have said, with the illusion of separation is fear. When one is overwhelmed by fear it is because they feel alone, unloved. I assure you that never are you alone, nor unloved. I would encourage them to pray, to ask for guidance. You, of course, can pray for them and hold them in the light of the divine. Linda, you personally have helped many with their pain with your healing words and insights. God bless you. You also have come to understand that each person has to take responsibility for their own feelings. One cannot do that for them. Such as in grief, have you not written about that yourself, Linda?

The anguish of grief is often not so much for the person who has left the earth life, but directed inward by the one who is left behind. They feel abandoned and filled with sorrow. It is also about the love that was not shared and expressed before death and the guilt feelings or shame one feels about the way they treated their loved one, is it not? You know by your experience with the earthly loss of Don, do you not? As you know, you had no issues with Don, you had an expressed love and understanding. But have you not seen others who loved Don, but yet had issues unsettled, unexpressed, and it has caused them pain and resentment as they mourn him? Have you not seen that in others who you have counseled and helped to heal in their own grief? You understand?

Linda: Yes, I do. I have often said that my grief has been much easier than I would have expected and I feel it is because I have no unresolved issues with Don, and the deep love between us was expressed moment to moment. There weren't things left unsaid, no regrets. My understanding that we do not die and my connection to the spirit world has been a great help to me. I try to share that understanding with others, but I also have learned that I cannot resolve their unresolved issues for them, as you just said.

Dr. Peebles: Uh, yes. That brings us back to the illusion of separation. If one believes at the heart level, at the conscious level, that one is a spiritual being, then one believes that there is no death. So why do you mourn for your loved ones? It is because of the illusion that they are no longer with you. Yes, they are not there in the physical sense, but their soul is very much with you, no matter where they reside, do you see?

And in regards to the unresolved issues you speak about, it is not too late for one to resolve issues. The lines of communication are always open.

Now, hopelessness and despair can immobilize. Depression is an act of denial. It is a retreat from life and is based on fear. In those quiet moments of the dark mind, is the time to call out to God. But one has to be willing to hear the answer. So you asked how to help someone in that state of hopelessness. It can only be done with love. When you shower your love on that person they cannot help but feel it. Even if it comes from your prayer when not in their presence. It is through the love which you send to them, which may help to tear down the illusion of separation they surround themselves with. But that is where your responsibility ends. Do you understand?

It is then that person's responsibility to take the love and allow it to reawaken their soul. Love will dissipate fear and pain. For many, it can be a struggle, a heavy challenge, to release fear and embrace love. Fear can bring confusion to the mind. Therapy can help to set the thoughts in order and break through the shell that the person has retreated into. Therapy comes in many forms. Often, it can be as simple as allowing one to express their pain and fear in words and having someone listen—listen with a loving and open heart. As I have already said, it can come from prayer. If one can reach out to the love of God and the angels, new understanding will come—and if surrounded with the power and love generated by prayer—it will touch that person at a soul level. Then the illusions of separation will begin to drop away but not until self-responsibility takes over.

Someone in a state of depression believes themselves to be a victim. They put the blame on others, circumstances, etc., and cannot see that it has been their own thoughts, perceptions of life around them, that has caused them to become the victim in their own mind. Every human being on planet earth has a tiny bit of depression, for that goes with separation, the illusion of separation.

But I also say to all of you, never are you the victim. You create your inner world, just as you create your outer world. In coming to understand self-responsibility, you come to understand that victimhood does not have to belong to you.

Linda: Dr. Peebles, many have trouble with this idea that we are never the victims. Can you elaborate more on that?

Dr. Peebles: Yes. Each of you first have to understand that it was your choice to come to earth to have experiences, lessons, to enable you to expand your spiritual awareness. You picked your parents and many of the experiences and events in your life for reasons of growth.

Maybe one needed more experience in understanding rejection and abandonment. In that case, they may have picked a mother who did not want a child to love, who was cold and distant, or a father who was working on his own personal issues of intimacy. Now each of them become a lesson for the other. Do you see? Also everyone's soul is not on the same level of spiritual growth. Maybe the father has only experienced one other life on earth and that life was filled with hatred and bigotry. So he is now slowly learning to understand and experience a new level of love and intimacy and he is filled with fear and anger of allowing love to enter his life, so his actions are abusive. Maybe the mother is on Earth to understand her past life when she, herself, was abused and abandoned. Now she is having a lesson in being the abuser or abandoner. And because the child wanted to experience rejection and abandonment, he chose those two as parents so it might be easier to experience and understand those things by having those two as parents.

Now, the understandings and spiritual evolution come from being able to experience these things and gain new perspective from them. That is the challenge, and often a difficult challenge. So, if you can look at life as a challenge, a lesson to be learned, by your own choice of circumstances, then you are able to see what a rich lesson of spiritual growth it can be for you. But if you look at those choices as if you had nothing to do with them, then you see yourself as a victim, and you become caught up in victimhood. But if you can have the perspective that this is growth for you and a lesson in motivations, not only of yourself but of others, then there is something to be gained by understanding that. It also teaches you that love begins within one's self, and that is also where forgiveness lays. Let's say you did grow up in an abusive family. What do you do with that? Do you continue the abuse within your new family as an adult? Or, do you generously give to your spouse and children the love you were denied? Those are the choices, the perceptions which are within your hands. Have you learned what it feels like to be rejected and do you ensure that you do not reject others with your behavior? Have you felt the aloneness of abandonment and do you give companionship and attention to others or do you turn away from those you love? It is your choice to react in either way. As the victim, you would probably choose to abuse, reject and walk away from those around you. As the creator, you would choose to look at your early life experiences as lessons of spiritual growth and ensure that you do not put others through what you had to endure as a child. If you have made the choice to be the creator, and let go of the victimhood, someone who had only known you as an adult, would probably have no idea of what you had gone through as that rejected child.

Remember, the choice of perception of each and every event in your life, belongs to you alone. It is yours to do whatever you wish with it. Your lessons belong to you as does the rate of spiritual growth. There is plenty of time, centuries upon centuries, upon centuries, to learn those lessons, and there are many challenges along the path to spiritual enlightenment.

So don't try to measure growth with some imaginary yard stick. You are where you need to be at any given moment. Trust in that.

4

INTIMACY, OUR GREATEST FEAR, OUR GREATEST CHALLENGE

"Oh, it is sweet—it is life evermore to breathe the beauty of love!"

—*James Martin Peebles, 1869*

As a humanitarian, James Martin Peebles often wrote of the need for universal love to be at the center of all things. In his book, *Seers of the Ages,* first published in 1869, he penned, "Love is not merely a white lily undulating upon embosomed waters, not an æolean harp murmuring music in the window, not the cooing of the turtle doves, but an active principle, a divine soul-emotion, the central magnet of our conscious existence. Just in the ratio of the soul's unfoldment, love becomes subjective, philosophic, idealistic and universal. Platonic love, blending with the fraternal, and enzoned by the infinite, is exalting beyond all heights of mortal perception."

Now we will examine Dr. Peebles' present view on intimacy which he has often referred to in his spiritual psychology as our greatest fear.

Dr. Peebles: It is such a paradox that since ancient time, man's innate drive has been to achieve intimacy, yet, it is his greatest fear. Why does he fear it? Because in order to achieve true intimacy one has to surrender to another. Give up control, so to speak. Yeah…surrender control. And within the breast of man, that idea of surrender stirs up anxiety and fear. One may believe that the search for security is foremost in the conscious mind, but the soul desire and need for intimacy prevails. With true intimacy, there is no need to *desire* security, for it is there. Secure within one's heart and secure within one's soul. But most often, one will run, as fast as a bunny rabbit, from a *threat* of intimacy. Why does one consider it a threat? Again, the fear of surrender, of giving up control. *Oh, if I give in to intimacy, good God!—I give up a part of me!* In order to achieve intimacy, one has to abandon the fear that something will be taken from him or her, and they will no longer be safe. This all plays into the illusion of separation.

When you deny yourself intimacy, the end result is pain because the desire for intimacy is a powerful force within your soul. So it begins a cycle—move away from intimacy—it brings pain; desire intimacy and without it—pain.

So begins the great challenge. How does one let down their guard to be able to achieve what they so desperately desire—intimacy? Look at a newborn baby, who has entered the world wholly dependant on his mother, or someone such as her, to provide him with all his needs—albeit food, comfort, security and love. There, is the greatest desire for intimacy. What happens to that same baby if he is denied intimacy? Does it not leave a scar upon him? His young heart cries out for an intimate relationship with another human—someone to hold him securely, to offer him love and comfort. Does not the heart of a child, an adolescent, an adult, cry out for the same? Is not the desire for love and intimacy always within the heart? Look deep in the eyes of a dying patient who is alone, isolated, in his last days on earth. Do you not see the longing for intimacy, for love? Do you not see the fear present in his eyes? Can you not hear the silent cry for some connection with another? Does he not long to have someone gently touch his hand, someone to give him a smile, someone to recognize that he is still alive?

The drive for intimacy is at a deep soul-level. So why does one fear it so much? Why do humans turn from it, whether it be an intimate relationship with their spouse or lover, with their child, with their neighbor, their community, or with the rest of the world—their fellow human beings? Fear! Fear!

In order to achieve intimacy, one has to release fear. One has to learn to appreciate the diversity, the differences, which are so much a part of life—whether it be a diversity of thought, likes or dislikes, or religious ideals, or social and cultural differences, etc. In allowing those differences in another, whether it takes place within your own family, or within your community, your country or the world, moves you one step closer to embracing true intimacy.

In order to achieve intimacy, it has to begin within yourself. And it begins with vulnerability. You have to allow yourself to be open to attack. *Attack*!—you say. Yes, attack.

That attack does not have to take place, so to speak, but you have to open yourself to the possibility. You see, when you are closed, invulnerable, it is because you feel that you are different, separate, from the other person. That is the illusion of separation. You are no different. Uh, your ideas may vary, may not be in tune, but you are a spiritual being, just like he is. Right? You see? And when you think you are different from another person, then fears arise. *Oh, that person does not like me...Look how he stares at me...He looks like a monster...*How would you feel if that person was thinking the same of you? If you knew those were his thoughts, would you not be on guard, feeling rejection, ready to attack him before he could attack you? But because you are connected and vibrationally a part of each other, he senses your discomfort. What if he is staring at you because he left his glasses at home and he cannot clearly make out your features from across the room and he thinks he may know you? But because of your illusion of separation and the fear that his actions have stirred up in you, you are on guard, feeling rejection, and ready to attack. See how silly? As he crosses the room and walks up to you, are you going to avoid him, or be ready to attack, or, are you going to welcome him with a smile? Of course, it is your choice. But what if you also left your glasses at home, and when he comes up to you, you see that it is your business associate? See how you allowed fear to rule. Instead, you could have accepted this person from the moment your eyes locked gazes and a fear of attack would not have been there. You would have been vulnerable—open to attack—but not *fearing* that an attack was about to happen.

Whether it be the intimacy of sexuality or the intimacy with someone who lives in another country—someone who you have never met, it is all the same. In order to achieve intimacy, one only has to open their heart to receive the echo of another. When two or more are gathered—intimacy can take place. But it only takes one to understand. If you open yourself to intimacy, then no matter what the response or the echo that comes back to you, intimacy has been achieved.

In the dropping away of illusion of separation, one is able to recognize again the face of God. It is the intimate relationship with God which allows one to understand that the God-connection is vital and powerful. The God-essence becomes again, a part of your heart/soul. As you recognize the God-essence within yourself, you will also recognize it in your fellow-man. It matters not, how different your life may be from his. For in that God-essence is the understanding that you are not different, not separate. Oneness returns to your conscious memory. You remember again who you are—a divine soul who is a particle of the Mind of God, and connected to every other human being, who, too, are divine souls.

Linda: Dr. Peebles, you mentioned that intimacy has to begin within. It really has to begin with that understanding that we are one with God, is that correct?

Dr. Peebles: Yes, yes it does. God is All. That includes you, me, and every other life form; the planets which make up the solar system; the stars that twinkle in the night sky, the expansive changing universe; the atoms; energy; the good, the bad and the ugly. Everything. God is complete, God is total. And all is contained within God.

So in understanding that concept, intimacy has no choice except to express itself. It is only when there is resistance to the idea that God is All and that each soul is contained within the divine source, that intimacy does not fully express.

But when intimacy is in effect, the God-essence showers every thought, every deed, and souls touch and merge. One moves again to God, and in that movement, expresses God in His completeness.

So the challenge, the greatest challenge for those in the Earth-school, is to recognize that intimacy begins within and you are the one who has to reach out to another, to the many, to the all. Do not wait for someone to come to you. You move to them, with your mind, with your heart, with your soul. If they turn from you, you have not failed. Do you see?

But you say, why do I bother?—They turn away from me. It matters not. *You* have achieved intimacy. *You* understand that you come from *love*. It is *their* illusion, *their* fear, which keeps them from connecting in an intimate way with you. So I say to you, reach out, touch, and in doing so, you allow yourself to be touched.

Linda: Dr. Peebles, would you talk to us of forgiveness. That seems to be a difficult area for most of us.

Dr. Peebles: Yes. Forgiveness, too, is a part of intimacy. In order to forgive, it takes an act of intimacy. Forgiveness is misunderstood. It does not mean that if you have been wronged by the actions of another that in order to forgive that person, that you have to agree that what they did to you was okay and approved of. No, it does not mean that. Forgiveness is an inward act just as intimacy is. It is allowing that person to be who they are, and allowing their perceptions to belong to them. It is *your* perception that matters. And in allowing your perception to change from feelings of rejection or anger, etc. and replacing it with allowance, loving allowance, then forgiveness manifests. Remember,

never are you the victim. You create your reaction. If you put expectations on another, or on the outcome of an event, then in all probability
you will be disappointed. If you had not placed any expectations, then
what a surprise at the outcome. You do not want demands, boundaries,
or limits on yourself, so do not move to put them on another.

So when you think of forgiveness, think of yourself. Let all expectations, all demands, all limits, drop away. Forgive yourself for your feelings of victimhood, hurt, anger, and release the resentment, anger or
other emotions you have bottled up or expressed toward another.
When that occurs, you will come to understand forgiveness. It will
bring you freedom of the heart—freedom from the control of another.
And you will realize that the power of the actions of that person no
longer is held over you. You regain your power. And the intimate act of
forgiveness is yours, always.

Linda: When someone has been the victim of some horrible violent
crime, or when someone is murdered, it must be very difficult for
either the victim of that crime or the victim's families to come to any
place close to forgiveness. How can that situation be made easier?

Dr. Peebles: By putting into effect the intimate act of forgiveness. Each
of you will be judged when you leave the earth plane. But it is not God
who judges. It is not the arch-angels. It is not your brother or sister. It
is *you*, yourself. When you come over here, you come with all your
consciousness, and you have to answer to yourself for all your actions,
deeds, and you will study all the things you did while in the body. All
the good, and all the bad. You will have to come to terms with that.
On occasion you may be shown in detail the effect you had on others,
both positive and negative. You will become your harshest judge as you
review your life.

The understanding that each has to answer for their behavior can
give comfort to those who are victims of horrific crimes. For many,
they feel that justice may not be done on earth. It may not in the eyes

of many, but the time will come when self-responsibility must come to be.

I know it is hard for many to see that the criminal lives in fear. Fear of intimacy. But he, too, cries out for love. He carries a heavy burden of the illusion of separation, the heaviest of anyone on Earth. He struggles in desperation to find some connection, and in his hunt, often, he moves further away from intimacy instead of drawing it closer to him. Some criminals find feelings of security and sanctuary behind the walls of a prison. When released from the safety of those walls, they panic, and fear overcomes them again. It can be a never-ending cycle of the need for intimacy, and the great fear of intimacy. In their fear, power over others may be the only thing that gives them relief from fear, albeit only momentary. As I have said before, much can be done to bring healing within the prison walls. But it will take a special brand of healing to achieve progress in what is called, rehabilitation. The focus has to change. The heinous criminal cannot be allowed to roam the streets and take out his fears and anger on society. He must be confined. But if it is understood that his illusions of separation are great and that he carries with him deep fears of that separation and deep fears of intimacy, then, possibly, movement can be made to lessen those fears, and through therapy, bring him closer to the God-essence.

Now back to forgiveness. To eliminate a life of pain that can result from feelings of victimhood, or powerlessness, if one can learn to let go, can add new thought, new perception, and understand that each and every person on earth all have illusions of separation and the need for intimacy, some much greater than others, then forgiveness can be easier. Forgiveness becomes an act of intimacy, nothing else. And intimacy takes only one to understand. Peace and healing will come when you take action to diminish the illusion of separation within the self. Only then.

5

THE FIRST PRINCIPLE, LOVING ALLOWANCE

o o o o o o o o o o o o o o o o o o o o o o o o o o o o o
"The divine principles—wisdom, love, truth."

—James Martin Peebles, 1869

When I read the earthly writings of Dr. Peebles I am awed by the similarity of the spiritual philosophy he held at that time and the philosophy he now relates to us from the other side.

Well over a hundred years ago, James Martin Peebles wrote about the differences between each of us, our individuality, not only as humans, but as carried into the world of spirit.

He had this to say: "Diversity is as much a law of the universe as unity, and each and all, whether on earth or in spirit life, aspect from their own plane of existence. This is the necessity of individuality.

"No two grains of sand, nor blazing stars, are precisely alike...so it is also with the mind, or rather the immortalized intelligences that people the world of spirits. Being in different states, influenced by different motives, members of different societies and occupying different spheres, they necessarily perceive the scenery of the higher life, and describe their employments there, in accordance with the idiosyncrasies of character, as well as with the variety and capability of their descriptive talents."

His acknowledgment that diversity was a universal law corresponds with what he now teaches—that we have to learn to love and respect the diversity and allow it to express.

The spiritual psychology that Dr. Peebles now presents to us here on earth, centers around three very important and sound principles. These three principles are the foundation of his teachings. Within these principles is wisdom; a truth that cannot be disputed; and love. They are essentially the same *divine* principles which Dr. Peebles believed to be of great importance while he was in the body.

The terrestrial Dr. Peebles also held the belief that God not only was everywhere but that each of us was a part of God and even with our diversity and individuality, we were all part of the greater whole. In his book, *Seers of the Ages*, he had this to say, "Full of trust, I consciously see God, the *Divine Energy*, everywhere,—pulsating in the growing corn, purpling in the vineyard, blushing in the peach, smiling in the sunshine, and awing us as we gaze into the infinite depths filled with stars, circling suns, and systems of universes."

The first of his three principles is *loving allowance*. It is an all-embracing concept and encourages every expression of man, praises every movement, gives reverence to the human experience as a consequence of the diversity of God's Expression on Earth. It *celebrates our differences*. One point of view amplifies another. We learn by our differences. We are not only enriched by those differences, but each of us enrich the world by the diversity of our individual thought, by our actions and perceptions, by our own priorities, our talents and skills. Loving allowance links us to every other man, woman and child on the planet in mutual respect and love. Is not the presence of God best expressed through diversity rather than sameness? Yet, how often do we turn from others who are not exactly like ourselves? How often do we fail to remember that we are all of God and that God is Everything?

If we consider that we are here on Planet Earth to gain new understandings and growth in our cycles of soul evolution, to move closer to the God-essence, to embrace unconditional love, to dissolve the illusion of separation, to remember again that we are spiritual beings, then we must first experience God as a living presence upon the planet, as nature and through nature—and that includes each of us. The presence of God, which permeates all of life, must be experienced as a spiritual presence that rejoices in all our unique contribution to the collective.

We must recognize God through every disguise, in every plant and insect, in every sunrise and moonrise, in every word and thought and deed, within the gaze of every man, woman, child, and animal upon Earth; we must feel His presence in all work and play, in song and dance and every artistic expression, in sexuality as well as spirituality, in every apprehension of the mind.

It's not an easy task to accomplish. But Dr. Peebles and his band of angels are with us to give us tools to aid in our life journey. Dr. Peebles' prescription for spiritual enrichment can enable us to "cure" our wounds, heal our hearts, and it provides preventive medicine.

So we will now look at the first of the three principles with the help of the good doctor.

Linda: Dr. Peebles, for many of us who have been lucky enough to have had contact with you, we have learned the value of the three principles which you teach. I've not only seen the effects of using the principles in my own life, but have seen, through friends, the positive effect the use of the principles have had on their lives. I would like to consider your first principle for this chapter. Would you elaborate on it for us?

Dr. Peebles: God bless you. Yes, Linda, we will speak of *Loving Allowance*. This principle, alone, is of the utmost importance. *Loving Allowance for all things to be in their own time and space, beginning with yourself.* It is the God connection. It comes first for a reason. Without a full understanding of this principle, the other two principles will fail. Let me explain. The second principle, *Increased Communication with all of life everywhere and with respect,* can only come about after the first principle, *Loving Allowance* is put into action. The third principle, *Self Responsibility, for you are the creator, never the victim,* will only come from an understanding of *Loving Allowance.*

Now, the three principles have to be used together, in tandem, but as I have said, it is the understanding of the first principle which allows for the effectiveness of the other two.

Loving allowance for all things to be in their own time and place, beginning with your *self.* How often do you allow for others against what is in your heart? How often do you give in, go against your personal agenda to make things easier for another? You say, that is okay—it keeps the peace, it gives loving allowance. But then, you are filled with resentment for being "forced" to allow another his way. You see how that does not work? The resentment builds and may not be expressed at the time but inside it churns around like the swirling waters of a tide pool and pulls you downward, or it churns and steams like the hot molten magma building in the underground crater of a volcano, slowly working its way toward the surface to explode in a violent outburst of heat and energy into the far reaches of the sky above. If you allow for the diversity of opinion, share with another your opinion without fear, allow the echo to take place, then move ahead with what is in your heart, you are then true to your *self.* There is no need for resentment, anger, unexpressed or expressed. You see?

Loving allowance has to first begin with the self. Only then, can it be generated to another. Allow, in a loving way, all things to be, in their own time and space. When you allow yourself to *be,* then every thing around you is okay from your point of view. But what if you take on guilt, retreat from your personal ideas, bottle up anger, hold on to events of the past, look at life with eyes of resentment, can you see how that will color the world you see. Remember, it is your own perceptions, your own thoughts, which become your canvas of life. It is you who holds the paint brush and strokes that canvas. It is always *your* painting.

No one is perfect. You would not be on the planet Earth if you were perfect. Graduation would have taken place. It is a life lesson to strive toward perfection, the perfection that the God-essence holds. In the struggle to reach perfection, many obstacles will have to be overcome. And I say to you, it is overcoming the obstacles, moving through and around them, which will bring you satisfaction and joy. When you look ahead, there will be other obstacles in front of you. Embrace them, do not fear them. As you hold them to your bosom, you will find that they will begin to dissolve from the warmth of your heart, and your path will open up again. *Oh, Dr. Peebles, you make it sound so easy,* you say. Yeah, Dr. Peebles does make it sound easy. When you can allow all of life to be, in its own time and place, and allow for yourself the same, it will be easy. That is the challenge for each of you, to come to that place of ease, to allow love for yourself, to let of go of all expectation of another, and of yourself, to give to another—all others—the allowance to be who they are, where they are, to allow them to walk their own path, while you are allowed to walk your own.

Loving allowance is not an earthly principle. It is a Godly principle. God makes no judgement, he allows for each of you to be, in your own time and space. He knows that at some time in your evolution you will reach Him. He gave each of you the gift of free-will. He allows, with love, your errors, your imperfections, your failures, just as he allows your successes, your truths, your talents. All He hopes is that you allow yourself the same, along with your brother, sister, and all His children.

When you come to the full understanding that you are a child of God, a spiritual being, then how can you not love yourself as He loves you? Loving allowance will then become a way of life for you. Allow yourself to be, in your own time and space. Allow for others to be, in their own time and place. And do it with love, L-O-V-E.

Forgiveness plays a big role in loving allowance. And it begins with self. If you can learn to forgive yourself then forgiveness of others comes automatically. It, too, becomes a way of life. As natural as the sunrise every morning. Each new dawning brings a new day. Each new forgiveness brings love. Each expression of love breaks through the illusion of separation. As the illusion falls away, intimacy becomes yours. And with intimacy comes unconditional love. And with unconditional love, is the God-essence. The spiral of love, moving in gallant force through the universe—spinning, turning, returning to Itself in all Its glory.

Linda: That's beautiful, Dr. Peebles. It brings to mind something you have said to us before, I don't remember the exact quote, but it was about the spiral being the fabric of eternity.

Dr. Peebles: Yes, I talked of the circle. The perfect circle moves in finite space, around and around in the same place. When you transform your circle into a spiral, you touch the fabric of eternity. It is the spiral which spins, gathering all it needs on its journey, never-ending. It is the DNA of life, it is love, never-ending, it is God-consciousness, the gossamer-threads which make up the cosmic All. It is the trinity of consciousness, soul and God, all as One.

Linda: Ah, again, beautiful. When I think of the spiral, never-ending, I cannot help but picture some of what we have seen out there in the universe—the spiraling, swirling nebula and galaxies—and, the helix of DNA.

Dr. Peebles: Yeah. Creation in all its splendor.

Linda: I know this is off the subject of loving allowance but your talk of the spiral, the circle and the trinity brought it to mind, so I will ask. Sacred Geometry seems to keep popping into my life and I would like to know what you may know about that, specifically, the tetrahedron.

Dr. Peebles: Ah, some science. Let me see here…As I have just said, the spiral is the fabric of eternity. The trine, the triangle, holds a sacred place, not only with the more modern belief held for two thousand years, of Father, Son and Holy Spirit, but back to the beginning of creation, with God, Spirit, and Man. Within that triangle is the connect-edness of all Three. If God is at the top, the tip of the triangle, the lines down each side connect Him with Spirit at one point and with Man at the other, and in turn, Man and Spirit are not only connected to each other, but to God. Now, at looking at the tetrahedron, we see it in all its dimensions—like what you call a hologram—no matter which angle we look upon it, we see God, Spirit, and Man. We see four dimensions or facets, but we really see the same. And from each facet, we see All. Now if you look at all the four faces of the tetrahedron there also becomes a finite point where God, Spirit and Man *stand together*. So here, too, as with the spiral, we see the fabric of eternity, the essence of creation. I suppose you could call all this Sacred Geometry, for it is the foundation of creation, but it is also something beyond what one would call scientific, and when one thinks of geometry, one thinks of science. It demonstrates the God-essence, the unconditional love, between God, Man and Spirit, and that all are not only part of the whole but part of each other. So sacred it is. Does that answer your question?

Linda: Yes it does. You're also saying that in looking into each dimension of the tetrahedron we are seeing, the same, no matter our position—this side of the veil or the other—God, Man and Spirit—all one, complete, and connected. And no matter, the perspective from which we gaze upon it. Is that right?

Dr. Peebles: Yes. The spiral, the triangle, the tetrahedron, all signify a higher truth and within the center of that truth is God. God is the creator of all. The triangle, and in turn, the tetrahedron, and other geometric forms based on that, symbolize spiritual Truth. God is complete but within that completeness is the essence of all that is—including man. But man is a spiritual being that has taken on a physical form, albeit only temporary. And within man is God. The energy of man, spirit, and God merge with one another, and out of that mix the greatest force in the universe, love, arises. That is, if it is not blocked by the mind of man. As we have spoken of, man in his physical cloak, is fighting to overcome the illusion of separation from God and spirit, and is struggling to overcome his fear of intimacy—intimacy with God, himself, and with others.

That is where Loving Allowance comes in again. Now, if one can fully take into his heart that he is, indeed, a spiritual being, than one cannot help but have loving allowance, unconditional love. You see? And if one truly believes that he is a part of a loving God, then, again, loving allowance is paramount in the mind and heart.

But what if one sees God as a punishing God, a judgmental God, will it not be difficult to see unconditional love at all? Yeah, the paradox. *God is not always loving, so why should I be so loving?* Might that not be the illusion of separation rearing its head? Or one might say, "I'm not worthy of God's love." God loves you, with all your faults, all your flaws, and all your failures. He does not see, except to see the beauty which he has instilled in every soul.

As each of you break through the illusion of separation you will learn to see with God's eyes. There is no failure, there is only growth.

What is growth? It is moving toward the God-essence, the God-consciousness, or Christ-consciousness as some may call it. Coming to a place when, from deep within the heart, from deep within the soul, you embrace all of life, including yourself, with unconditional love. When that is accomplished, you will intimately know the face of God.

But this movement toward God can only begin within. And it begins with Loving Allowance, for all things to be, in their own time and place, beginning with yourself.

As God loves you, you have to learn to love and celebrate yourself. And through that celebration of self, you will understand the celebration of a spiritual being, who has come into physical life for experiences, for lessons of growth, for soul purpose, and to be part of a much greater universal experience. And as you recognize that spiritual being cloaked within the physical form, you will recognize the other spiritual beings who occupy planet Earth, and you will remember why you are there. The physical form will fall away before your eyes and you will recognize the soul of another, and another, and another. And you will again remember that you are one and the same. God, spirit and man, all part of the whole, God's Whole.

Every thought within your mind, expressed or not, has an impact upon that Whole. Every action, positive or negative, has an impact upon that Whole. Every smile given to another, every hug, every tear that rolls down a cheek, every physical abuse inflicted, every act of evil expressed, every war fought with another, every kind gesture, every expression of love, has an effect on that Whole. Would it not be a beautiful world if only good thoughts and unconditional love filled that Whole? Yes, it would be. But, planet Earth is a study in relation-ships—relationships of every kind and shape—and it is a study in the illusions of separation. That is your journey, as you move along the path of physical life. You have entered upon that journey for a reason, to understand how the illusion of separation can be whittled down, like a branch you have found along the riverbank and patiently pull away the bark with your knife to have a new and beautiful object emerge from the wood. And would it not be dull, if every relationship, every contact with another, was the same? Would you learn anything about yourself, about another, if all was alike? What if there was no conflict of thought, if all ideas were the same, no inspiration, no creative expression? What if love and sexuality were expressed in rote, no romance, no excitement? What if there was no ambition, no dream allowed of something better, no reason to educate yourself? What if life held no challenges? What if there was neither pain nor joy? What would you learn about yourself?

Linda: I see what you mean. It would not be an "opportunity for growth," as you say.

Dr. Peebles: Yes, right. And would it not be boring, stagnant, just like the perfect circle, moving round and round in finite space, caught in the same place, nothing added to it as it turns, never expanding, never growing, never changing. Now God is ever changing, always expanding, always adding to Himself, or Herself, as the symbology of the spiral of eternity signifies.

Linda: Herself…I always have a little trouble thinking of God as a *her*, although I realize that God embodies both the female and male energy.

Dr. Peebles: Yes, you do find that a little difficult to accept, Linda, as many do. For you, it is a personal battle of male strength verses female strength. As we have talked before, you came into this life with a wee bit of resistance to accepting the idea that you are female. You have been a male many times before in other lifetimes, and you have respect for your male side; you knew the male to be strong but you also knew the male to be weak. You still carry with you high admiration of the male strength even though you feel, and I might say, *know*, deep within your soul, that the female is strong, and that the female strength can sometimes be measured above the male, do you not?

Linda: (I have to say, this brought me quite a chuckle). Yes, Dr. Peebles.

Dr. Peebles: Yes. You also know the balance of male and female energy and the importance of that. And you admire that within a person—both the male and female. You love to see the sensitivity in the male, and you love to see the strength in a woman, am I not right?

Linda: Yes.

Dr. Peebles: Then, you see, God as He/She is a perfect balance of male and female, so perfect that one cannot measure any difference. One side is not stronger than another, one side is not weaker than another, one side is not more sensitive than another; the whole of God is blended in perfect balance with love permeating every fiber of His/Her Being. But that love is ever-expanding, ever-growing. So, the essence of God is All, All there Is and All there will Ever Be.

◆   ◆   ◆

For some, it may be hard to accept the idea that everything is contained within God. That's okay. That is what diversity means. Different points of view. Some believe that there is no God, that's okay, too.
Each of us are on our own journey and with the free-will we have, we
can choose to see life as we wish. As Dr. Peebles has pointed out, it is
our canvas and we hold the paint brush, and we can paint our picture
any way we want.

Some believe that God does not exist, that life has no purpose, that
there was no creator who brought this world into existence. It appears
to be a depressing view but with loving allowance it becomes a necessary view and valid for those who hold it on their journey.

The majority of Americans do believe in a loving "father" God with
whom some form of a personal relationship can be achieved, usually
through prayer and devotion. But even for all of those, their concept of
God and the Divine, is diverse. To some degree, many of us will then
resist the notion that God is All, depending on how literal is our inter-
pretation of holy scriptures and biblical creation doctrine. Since most
of us have been encouraged by our religious practices and beliefs to
view ourselves as separate from God and unworthy of God unless and
until we are raised by grace and made worthy, it can be a difficult
bridge from *God the Father* to *God the All, Including Me.*

So with religious or spiritual views, as well as other views on life, it
becomes a personal view, a truth each of us searches for within our own
quiet minds, and in our own ways, but in putting the first principle of
angelic wisdom, loving allowance, into action we acknowledge diversity, we allow it to be, in its own time and place. And in allowing
another's point of view we do not have to feel threatened by it. It does
not have the power to change one's own thinking, although, it may
give one something new to think about and consider.

◆   ◆   ◆

Linda: Can you give us some more examples of putting loving allowance into action within relationships?

Dr. Peebles: Yes, we would be happy to. What is a relationship? It can mean many things. It can be the relationship between parent and child, between spouses, between lovers, between neighbors, between co-workers, between man and nature.

For your purpose here, we will look at a few relationships. We will begin with parent and child. Earliest memories that one has, go back to early childhood. The infant, in his innocence and purity, looks to the adult to give him safety, sanctuary, and love. The infant, as he grows a little older, is filled with desire for exploration and new experiences. But often his desires are thwarted by the parent, often for reasons of his safety from harm or danger. It is the role of the loving parent to allow, with love, and protection, opportunity for exploration and new experiences. So with loving allowance, the parent sees that the toddler has opportunity to explore and experience in the confines of safety. A simple example of loving allowance. The toddler is allowed to be.

Now another example of a relationship is man's relationship with nature. You are out walking through the woods and the landscape is pristine. There is a gentle breeze blowing through the trees and birds are singing their songs from their perches among the branches, you sense the presence of deer in the meadow not far beyond you. You stop and drop a shell into the rifle you carry. You become a hunter, for no reason except the joy of the kill. You aim the rifle at one of the gathered deer and you pull the trigger and watch as the deer scatter and one falls to the ground with a thud. As you approach the deer, you hear one last gasp of air escape from him, his eyes still holding the startled stare as death stopped him in his tracks. You, the intruder, the killer, have taken from this life form the right to be, in his own time and place.

You have not given respect or loving allowance for him to be. And you have taken his life only to satisfy your own ego.

Instead, you could have continued your walk through the woods, enjoyed the song birds, watched the deer grazing in the meadow, had reverence for the beauty of all life forms, and loving allowance for all things to be, in their own time and place.

Now, we will give another example of a common scenario. Your point of view differs greatly from that of your business partner. You hold common goals but this difference of opinion can result in a change in the efforts to reach those goals. So what do you do? You communicate with each other with respect. You present your point of view and you *listen* to his point of view. If it appears that he is not listening to you, you again repeat your point of view. If after this exchange of ideas take place and neither of you are willing to change your perspective, then next comes consideration of your goals. In examining these goals with a fresh mind, might there be a way to reach those goals on an altered path? After much discussion, it is decided that your individual path to the goals is too much in contrast to mutually reach them. So then, with allowance for the other point of view, along with your own, a decision is made to break up the partnership and each follow your own path.

Therein lies the secret of relationships. Loving allowance for another to follow their own path. It makes no difference if their path takes them away from you, or in a direction you feel is filled with danger, or in a direction you have no understanding of.

Within the fabric of this first principle, is allowance to the fullest expression. It does not mean forcing your will upon another, imposing your ideas as they were the only ones that existed, or controlling one with power and force. It does not mean giving up your moral stand, nor retreating from your ideals. It means loving allowance, for all things to be in their own time and place, beginning with yourself. It means letting go of expectations, control. It means welcoming another point of view, celebrating the differences, anticipating with joy the echo, releasing fear, putting forgiveness into action, and living life with joy and love.

Loving allowance means striving to live your life with the God-essence at the center of your heart. It is the knowing that God, Man and Spirit are One.

It is the understanding of this first principle which then flows into the other two. Only with Loving Allowance at the center of the three principles will Increased Communication and Self-responsibility have any meaning or value.

Linda: Dr. Peebles, when you were on Earth you wrote in one of your books that the divine principles were wisdom, love, truth. I have used that as an opening quote to this chapter. I see those divine principles within your three spiritual principles. Any comment about that?

Dr. Peebles: Ah, yes. My spiritual beliefs and philosophy have not altered much since my days on Earth. I did learn a lot during those many years, thanks to my contact with the spirit world during most of that time. Much of what I learned came from them. I was lucky to have had great insight and inspiration offered to me from those on a level of increased spiritual understanding. I integrated that knowledge into my writings and teachings. At times, I could be overbearing with the pen and with the voice. In fact, most insistent with that overbearance. That expressed insistence kept life from being too dull, I might say. It kept the spiritual fires burning in me, and I do admit that despite the frustration I often endured, I found great satisfaction in expressing my views to the world.

Regarding my earthly observation of the divine principles. Yes, you might say that those divine truths are within my current principles. If you look at Loving Allowance, Increased Communication and Self-responsibility, you see love, of course, in loving allowance, and within increased communication with all of life everywhere and with respect, dwells wisdom, and in understanding self-responsibility, never are you the victim, always the creator, is an understanding and expression of truth.

So, in what I once called the divine principles, and what I now call the three principles of spiritual growth and enrichment, hold the same divine truth, only expressed in a somewhat different way.

But the love of God which is expressed in the embodiment of Man, Spirit, and God, is the center of All That Is. That is where you realize the Divine.

6

THE SECOND PRINCIPLE, INCREASED COMMUNICATION

o o o o o o o o o o o o o o o o o o o o o o o o o o o o o

"The more you increase your communication, the more present you will know the pleasures of Earth."

—*The grand spirit, Dr. Peebles*

The second principle of angelic wisdom presented to us by Dr. Peebles has a much broader meaning than one would think at first glance. When we think of increasing our communication, we think of speaking out with our feelings and ideas. It is that, but from the point of view of spirit, it goes way beyond that simple understanding.

In holding within our heart the first principle, loving allowance, as we examine the second principle, we will come to understand how vital loving allowance is to effectively putting to use this principle.

The definition of communication is a sharing of ideas, a giving or exchange of information, by talk, writing, gestures or signals and, of course, in today's modern world we have communication available through electronic means such as the telephone, television and radio waves, and the World Wide Web. These technological advances have, indeed, made it a small world.

But there has also been an upswing in another type of communication that reaches beyond our world into another dimension. And that is communication with the world of spirit which has taken on many forms. It is not a new communication, it has gone on since the beginning of time.

Recent polls of Americans tell us that nearly seventy percent believe in angels and that more than thirty percent have felt the presence of an angel and nearly fifty percent believe they have their own personal guardian angel.

We all know the power of prayer and recent scientific studies have validated that power.

A growing number of people are communicating with their angels and finding inspiration and comfort in doing so. For some, their angel may be a sainted angel, for others, a loved one who has made the transition to the other side.

Still others communicate, through mediumship, with entities of a higher nature, some who have been in the body, others who have not.

I personally believe that this type of communication with the spiritual world is increasing as the world moves into a renewed spiritual understanding and awareness. I do not hold any apocalyptic view of this. I believe it to be a natural movement in the scheme of things, a natural evolution.

It appears that in this century, science along with religion, has had us bound to their dogma, and we have begun to throw off the restraints in search for answers they have not given us. I have to applaud many in the scientific and medical world who are publicly stepping forward with spiritual understanding. The many studies which have been done on subjects such as near-death experiences, past life regression, healing, prayer, tend to enforce and give credibility to the idea that we are spiritual beings. I look forward to what scientific studies will uncover in the coming years. I believe it will be a spiritual awakening never before experienced.

Ten years or more ago, Dr. Peebles had spoken to us about the coming increase in contact with the spirit world. He had told us that more and more people would be having experiences which would validate the existence of spirit. He said that communication with the other side would become a normal, acceptable way of every day life and that the illusion of separation would become thinner—in other words, the veil between worlds would become more transparent.

I see that happening. I have spoken to many people who have had mystical experiences. One cannot help but notice the upsurge in the hunger for spiritual material which is being filled by the publication of many books on spiritual subjects, everything from angels, miracles, near-death experiences, the body/mind/soul connection, and aliens, and which also has found its way onto the television and movies screens with great success.

Intercommunication between the two worlds, our earthly world and the world of spirit, is taking place. In 1859, Dr. Peebles had this to say about the intercommunication between the worlds.

"Not only is it possible, but *probable*; for the spirit relieved of its gross earth garments, retains all its faculties, forces, mental characteristics and moral qualities. It is a substantial, organized, individualized and conscious entity, living, thinking, reasoning and loving, the same as before the transition. Pure love is imperishable and cannot cease—immortal and cannot die, and would not the mother, freighted with those warm-gushing emotions peculiar to her affectionate nature, delight, though in *spirit spheres*, to watch over her children? Would she be *herself*, or would heaven be such to her in *reality*, if she could not? Would not the good father rejoice in being a counsellor to his sons in earth-land?—and free to roam the universe would not the wisely ordained law of parental attraction oft call into their presence? The spirit world is not located afar in some infinitely remote region. It is all around us, as is the atmosphere we breathe; and intercourse between spirits *in* the body and *out* of it, is just as *probable*, and natural also as the oceanic commerce between America and the isles of the Pacific."

Dr. Peebles also believed that intercourse between worlds was certain. He quoted many biblical incidents supporting communication with spirit, including those of Jesus, John, Samuel, Saul, Daniel, Abraham, Jacob, Moses, Manoah's wife, Elijah, Zachariah, Mary, the Marys at the tomb of Jesus, Peter in prison, Paul, James, and "nearly all scriptural characters," and asked the question, "When did these spirit appearings—this intercourse cease? How dare the Christian affirm that it has, when the great master *medium*, or 'Mediator between God and man,' declared that he would be with 'them to the end of the world.'"

Dr. Peebles' personal experiences made him a believer. He continued, "I have seen *tables, books,* and other *materials* move without physical contact, also tambourines, violins and guitars sail rapidly around a room by some unseen power, discoursing all the time delightful melodies. I have heard the voice of my Indian friend, Powhatten, and other spirit voices as distinctly as I ever heard the human. Have seen the *spirit-form,* grasped the *spirit-hand,* felt the gentle *spirit-touch,* and feasted upon the most enchanting *spirit-music,* when there was no individual in the earth-form near me. These facts appealed to my senses of *seeing, hearing and feeling,* and I know them to be actual occurrences, if I *know anything* that transpires in my presence."

The mighty hand of James Martin Peebles penned his fast-held beliefs and his indignation with the idea that spirit communication should cease because some church mind said it should be so. He wrote, "Spiritual beings are daily and nightly descending to communicate with, and minister to, their mortal brothers," an axiom he still holds.

He also had insight into the ever-present search for spiritual understanding when he wrote, "Humanity is pleading, yearning for knowledge. Inquirers are still asking, 'If a man dies shall he live again? And if he live why may we not *know* it?'"

And the search for knowledge goes on.

◆　　◆　　◆

Just as I had finished writing the above opening to this chapter and was ready to begin my dialogue with Dr. Pebbles, my telephone rang. It was a friend. He told me he had just had something happen to him that he wanted to share with me. His voice was tinged with emotion as he explained, "I'm not sure what just happened a half hour ago, but I know it did happen."

Before I go into what he experienced on this October Sunday afternoon, I want to give some background so you will understand the full impact this had on him.

He is a man in his sixty's, a poet and author. He holds a Ph.D. in Metaphysics: Theology, Philosophy, and Mythology, and counsels in Behavioral Psychology, specializing in alcohol and drug recovery. When a young man, he was ordained in the Benedictine Order of Catholic Priests and left the Order after several years. He had also served as an Army combat medic during the Korean War.

A recovering alcoholic, he has endured more grief in this life than many. The previous year had been difficult for him. Within the prior year he has had to deal with the break-up of a relationship with the woman he loved, two major surgeries, and then a diagnoses of cancer. It has been overwhelming for him and he's had a difficult time dealing with all this. Many of his past grief issues have come up again, his first being the death of his mother when he was nine. Her death followed her agonizing three year struggle with cancer.

When his cancer was discovered he spoke to me, on more than one occasion, about his feelings that he could not go on. Every day had become a painfully emotional struggle for him. He was having great difficulty letting go of his six year relationship and, for a time, seemed to be in denial in taking any responsibility for the break-up. I talked to him of Dr. Peebles' three principles.

In the two weeks prior to our Sunday afternoon phone conversation, he had taken a big step forward in his emotional struggles. He had also begun radiation treatment. He was searching deeply within to heal not only the physical but all the emotional baggage which had burdened him for years upon years. He had been doing some heavy prayer and affirmation work. He and I talked often of his need to come to terms with and release all his past emotional baggage and to now turn his focus on his physical healing. At times, I would give him insight that I know came from beyond me. More than once, he asked me to repeat what I had just said, and I really couldn't because it was as if the words had just flowed through me and were not really a part of my own consciousness.

About a month before he had told me of a dream he had. He said he was aware of a spiritual being who said to him, "You ain't finished yet." I knew within the deepest part of me that those words came from Don. Even though *ain't* would not have been an ordinary conversational use by Don—he would have used it for emphasis, I was sure of that. I told my friend I believed that Don gave him that message. He replied that he had felt the presence of Don around him. Prior to that day, and more than once, I had asked Don to help our friend through this but I also knew it would not take my asking for Don to be with him—he would be there for his friend to help in whatever way he could. In my prayers, I also asked God to surround him with His love and light—and prayers were being sent to him by other friends of ours.

About two weeks after he had this message in the dream, he started his radiation therapy. After the first treatment he was not feeling well. It had left him nauseous and drained. He had awakened that night with abdominal cramps and was crying out to Jesus for comfort. He told me that he "felt a presence and it was as if there were arms holding me, giving me comfort."

So, on this October Sunday as I was sitting at my computer writing about spiritual communication, four hundred miles away, this friend was experiencing communication first hand. Feeling exhausted, he had laid down to rest and was in that in-between state, not really asleep, still aware, when he saw a shadow of a figure and then became aware of a bright light surrounding that shadow. The light became brighter and it flared out from the figure and he could not clearly see the figure itself as the radiating light was too bright. Then he heard the words, "*I am the loving presence of the Christ within you.*" He was then told that he would remember all that was said to him and was to write it down.

While he read to me what he had written, my whole body was covered in goose bumps (what I call my "knowing" bumps) and my eyes filled with tears. His voice was full of emotion as he read the words and had to stop a time or two during the reading. My first response when he finished, was "Oh, my God, that *was* Jesus." (As I write this my goose bumps are back!—and my eyes are moist.)

His voice was so choked with emotion that he could barely speak. He tried to describe to me again the bright light and the love and comfort he felt as it was happening. He said when he began writing the words he had heard he could hardly write fast enough—and keep up.

The poetic message he wrote that we both felt had come from Jesus was absolutely beautiful. It conveyed that Jesus was there to comfort and give him strength, and that He had always been there. Even though he gave me permission to use the poem in my book, because it was such a personal message to him, I feel it not proper to present it here; but trust that the words were so very beautiful, poetic, and overflowing with unconditional love.

Sometimes, out of the darkest moments of our lives, comes love, peace and healing in all its beauty!

◆   ◆   ◆

Linda: Hello, Dr. Peebles. It's time for your input on your second principle, Increased Communication.

Dr. Peebles: God bless you. Yes, Linda, the second principle: Increased Communication with all of life everywhere, and with respect.

Ah, many of you say, "Oh Dr. Peebles, that is an easy one. We just open our mouth and speak." Yes, you do, but it is much more subtle than that. It is not only what you say, but how you say it, in all the finite and infinite expressions. It is the way you present your message. Is it presented with respect? Is it presented with loving allowance, without restriction or expectation of what the echo may be which is returned to you? Are you perched on the edge of your chair in joyous anticipation of the response or have you said your piece and hurriedly turned away, fearing the echo that will return to your ears?

Have you spoken, without one wee bit of concern for how your words will be received by another? *I don't care, There! I have said it! That is what I think, like it or not!*

But Dr. Peebles, I have increased my communication. Yeah. It has been increased—but has it been increased with respect?

As you have loving allowance for all things to be, and show respect as you increase your communication—your words may be heard with a greater impact and understanding. They will not be taken as attack.

How will someone take your words and ideas if you stand rigid with hands on hips, a cold expression on your face, as you say, "But I do like you." Will you be believed? How often do you close off your mind to the words of another? *I do not want to hear your point of view so I will not listen.* Then you insist that your point of view be heard—and you yell loudly, expressing *your* view with anger and rage—and insisting that the other person disregard their view and respect only yours.

It happens all the time, in big ways and in little ways. It happens within families, within neighborhoods and within governments.

Would it not be better to be honest with your view, but to also honestly accept a different point of view as being just as valid. You can say, "I do not see it the same as you for these reason...." Now, the other may not want to agree with your reasons, but you have acknowledged their point of view while not surrendering your point of view and you have done so with respect, have you not?

Within the illusions of separation is a fear of communication. You believe that another may not understand you if your views are different than his, albeit religious, social, or ideology. You also want to believe that another with a different point of view, albeit religious, social, or ideology, is not like you in any regard. But as you break through the illusion of separation, and give loving allowance, then you release the fear of communicating with someone with a different point of view. You will learn that diversity is a joy to encounter.

Now, sudden increased communication can be seen as an assault, especially if it is done without respect. You say, we will increase our communication by marching into that country—or your own living room—with our weapons in hand, and we will show them what we believe to be the truth. War is an increase in communication. But so is an attempt to sit down at a table with your so-called enemy and break bread as you discuss your diverse opinions. Of course, events do not always allow for a peaceful discussion of diversity, especially if lives of innocent people are at stake. And at times like that, force may be implemented which tends to further the illusions of separation.

Sometimes force does become necessary but generally it is not. You may say, well that is only my government assuring the safety of others. But don't look to the government, look within your own heart. It is there and only there where the massive illusion of separation can begin to vanish.

Have you not spoken out for peace, within your family, within your community and within your world? Have you not spoken out to eliminate weaponry? Yet, have you not turned away from your homeless brother who is begging for a dollar; turned from the emotional pain of another; refused to discuss the different point of view of another; used implied threat, or outright threat to get your way?

Have you not often increased your communication without even a hint of respect? Now I do not say to you that your own point of view is not valid, but I do say to you to ignore another's differing view, to not listen to the expression of that view with respect, is to invalidate every view except your own. Need the other point of view change your point of view? No. But in allowing the echo, in allowing the unique view of another to be expressed, it can be a delightful opportunity for growth. There is a little truth in everything. *But, Dr. Peebles, that is not my truth.* No, it may not be, but if you listen carefully you may see a speck of truth in another's view. And, that speck may soon grow within your mind to allow for you to see things a little differently. The new under-standing you may gain is growth—in all its beauty.

Linda: How does one increase communication when the other refuses to listen?

Dr. Peebles: Ah, yeah, a challenge. You pick a quiet time, consider again your point of view. Review it. Does it need revision? Present it again, without malice, without expectation of the echo that will return. If you cannot do it in person, pick up a pen and paper and express it in prose. Before you lick that stamp and send it off, read it again. Is every word expressed with respect? Does it come from your heart? Does it come from love? If so, then you are ready for the echo. If you do not hear an echo, or even if that echo bounces off the walls with anger and rage, or hysteria, you have done your part. You have increased your communication with respect. You have given your point of view and you are open to receive the point of view of another.

Through the faculty of increased communication many doors may open for you. If you remain silent, how will another know your view? And if others catch a glimpse of a little bit of truth within your view then it may enable growth. You see? And often when respect is given, it may be returned. Not always, but often.

As you learn to increase your communication, you also increase your sense of community. But community means getting along by allowing diversity. You are now moving into the Aquarian Age which has at its center, truth seeking. It will be a search for truth and a letting go of bias. It will bring forward an increased attitude of community. But within that search for truth, there will be ups and downs, and bumps on the road. It is a splendid opportunity for growth. It will be a new awakening for many.

In recent years you have experienced this new movement. It will continue, and at times, may dizzy you, but it will bring forward many lessons to learn and understand, and will be an exciting time for spiri-tual growth. Look forward to it.

Within this movement will come an unfoldment of new under-standing and awareness. You will find a dropping away of bias and prejudice, you will experience moments of truth never before experi-enced, you will understand your spiritual self at a much deeper level, and others will be afforded that same understanding which you give to yourself.

Now, within this principle, we speak of increased communication with all of life everywhere. Life is made up of the human, and all the creatures who roam the earth. That includes the birds who sing for you and nibble at your garden; the four-legged animals who you have domesticated, and the ones who roam wild; the insects that you swat away as they buzz around your head; the bountiful vegetation which covers the land; and the many life forms who live in community with you on Planet Earth; and, it includes the Planet Earth, herself. She is alive and vital. All of it deserves respect.

Have you talked to a tree recently and told him how startling and impressive his brightly colored leaves are? Have you told the beautiful wild daisy in the field how beautiful she is? Have you spoken to the fish who swims in the water and told him how sorry you are that you have allowed his fresh water to become polluted? Have you asked the ants who have invaded your kitchen to find their way to the outdoors? Have you blessed the rich soil which allows your garden to produce food for you? Have you smiled at the stranger who passes you on the sidewalk?

Those are a few examples of how you can increase your communica-tion with life.

Respect comes from the heart as does love. With loving allowance for all things to be, in their own time and place, and increasing your communication with respect for all life everywhere, you have incorpo-rated self-responsibility. If you take personal responsibility for your place upon the planet, and understand that you are a integral *part* of the planet, then how can you not love and respect all of life everywhere and in every form?

That brings us back to the God-essence. If all is of God, including yourself, then communication with God is only natural. And so is communication with one another, each a part of God—and again, a spiritual being. And we, on this side of the veil, are spiritual beings. It is all one gigantic world, and only endures an *illusion of separation—separation* from God, or man, or spirit. So why would one not expect communication to take place with *all* within that gigantic world?

Many of us on this side of the veil are eagerly awaiting your communication. We often come to you in your dreams, and we also come to you when you ask for guidance or support in your prayers, meditations or waking state.

When you reach out your hand, we take it in ours and dance the dance of angels. We love to give you an echo, because in that echo you can hear yourselves, you can be energized, and moved in your hearts and souls. It is at that moment that the dance of love begins and within that dance you have declared permission to shout your truths and sing out your songs.

7

THE THIRD PRINCIPLE, SELF RESPONSIBILITY

o o o o o o o o o o o o o o o o o o o o o o o o o o o o o o o

"Men are the architects of their own hells; they reap what they sow."

—James Martin Peebles, 1879

One of the crucial points of Dr. Peebles' spiritual psychology is bound into the idea that all of us, each in our own way, are continually creating our own process. He tells us, "You are forever the eternal creator, never the victim."

Some of us are undoubtedly uncomfortable with that idea because it puts the responsibility back into our own hands. How often we may want to retreat from responsibility, but Dr. Peebles reminds us that we are creating ourselves, our own reality, our own heavens and hells. That is a sobering idea and if it is true, then there is no escape, even if we choose to disbelieve it.

Victimhood has become a way of life for many. If we are hurting and feeling abused from some pain of our own creation, we tend to find comfort in the illusion that we have been victimized. How often do we blame others for our reactions, forgetting that it is *our reaction* and that we *could* respond in a variety of ways? And why do we often "ignore" that we may have played a part in creating the situation? We do have a choice in how we perceive and react to any and all situations and events.

Since Don's death, I have come to understand how important our choices can be. We shared a very special love and a deep bond. When he and I talked of the eventuality of his death before mine because he was several years older than I, I would tell him there was no way I could go on living without him. He would often smile and tell me, "Oh, yes you can." Just thinking of life without him made my heart ache. So when his death came unexpectedly, I soon knew I had a choice. I could retreat from life and go off in some dark cave and wait to die, or I could choose to go on living. I chose to go on, and to find joy again, partly because I knew how much he would want that for me, and partly because my will to live was still as strong as ever. Much of the joy I find now in life without him is wrapped up with the beautiful memories he has left with me, and they will reside deep within my heart forever.

Over the years, I have watched love relationships of friends disintegrate. As an observer, I have also noticed how difficult it has been for each of the parties to take responsibility for their part in the breakdown of the relationship. What is often heard is "she said," or "she did," and from the opposite member of the relationship—"he said," or "he did." Some tend to take on the role of victim. What appears to be missing is *truth*, and within that truth lies responsibility.

The breakup of any relationships is never easy and grief is a very real result, even for the one determined to end the relationship. Grief issues have to be dealt with because until they are, they will remain and tend to color one's life in negative ways.

I have learned from the teachings of Dr. Peebles that all life experiences are part of our growth, and as he would say, "Great opportunities for growth!" Sometimes it may be very difficult to see things in just that way, especially if one is submerged in sorrow, pain, resentment, or anger. And at other times, we may come to see how it came to be a period of tremendous growth for us.

So let's take a look at how we can learn to take responsibility for our own actions, thoughts, perceptions, and reactions—and accept that we are the creator of our lives, never the victim.

Wow! With that acknowledgment comes one hell of a sense of self-responsibility!

◆   ◆   ◆

Linda: Hello, Dr. Peebles. I'd like to review your third spiritual principle.

Dr. Peebles: God bless you. Ah, yes. The third principle is Self-Responsibility, for you are the eternal creator, never the victim.

Now, if one can learn to put self-responsibility into action, and reaction, the life experience can become more rewarding.

In order to do this, it can be another of life's great challenges. Is it not easier to put blame on others, shrink from one's responsibility? This is especially true if the illusion of separation is strong within the mind and heart.

But in order to understand self-responsibility one has to embrace the first principle, loving allowance—beginning with self. When you can allow yourself to be—you will recognize that it is only *you* who has control of your life. And in accepting that, it will be only natural that you take all responsibility for your actions and reactions. Your reaction does not depend on another. It is *yours* alone. You may want to say, *I did not create that response—that echo.* But when you examine it carefully, you will see that some little bitsy thing you may have done gave you the result that occurred. And by acknowledging your responsibility you can then change what needs to be changed within your own mind and heart. You see?

If you feel the victim—that you took no part in the outcome, then that is exactly what you will be—the *victim*. And within victimhood, is escape from self. It is denial of self. It is helplessness and hopelessness.

It is self-doubt, and lack of self-worth. By escaping self, you escape from life. You re-enforce the illusion of separation and retreat from intimacy with all life. The Christ-love falters within your heart. The illusion of separation grows larger, and self becomes smaller. You see?

By understanding that you are, indeed, the creator of your life, it returns power, respect and love—beginning with self. The illusion of separation then becomes smaller and self becomes larger. Self-doubt leaves, and self-worth returns. You no longer feel helpless or hopeless as self-empowerment returns.

But the paradox. By claiming your power you also have to claim self-responsibility for your life and, in doing so, you claim responsibility for your every action, thought and deed.

That is a big one—*thought*. Your every thought has a reaction. But you say, *No one knows my thoughts except me*! Wrong. Thoughts are real. Once they are put into form within your mind, they are an energy, and energy moves and energy does. They are a force, a reality, and become a part of the universe. Of course, your actions and deeds have not only an impact on others but on self. And often, more on self, than others.

Linda: Will you explain what you mean by "more on self," Dr. Peebles?

Dr. Peebles: Ah, yeah. When we talk of the energy of thought, that energy begins within. It has an impact on the mind, but also on the body, does it not? If the thought is ugly, then ugliness permeates through every cell within the body. If the thought is beautiful it also permeates every cell of the body. Which kind of thought would you prefer to have impact on your body?

Now, as a result of your action and deed, the echo which returns to you may be one of anger. That anger has an impact on your mind and heart. It may lead to anger within yourself, or heavy stress within the body. If your own action could be called inappropriate, and even if you do not receive an echo, just your own behavior alone can impact your mind and body with stress and anger. Where does that stress and anger go? *Into every cell of your body.* The result will be dis-ease within the immune system and with dis-ease of cells within the body can come an attack. And so, real disease manifests within the living universe of the physical body. So, it is turned inward even though it was designed to go outward. You see?

Linda: Yes. The idea that we create our own disease is one that many find so hard to accept.

Dr. Peebles: Yes. It is hard to accept because in doing so, one has to take responsibility. But you must also remember that when you come there to school-earth you come with many lessons in mind. Sometimes, a particular disease may be a part of the lessons of growth. It may not be that you purposely choose to create a particular disease within yourself, but that your fears and angers may enable the disease cells to take a hold on your body. And the battle begins. It can often be a time for real understanding of self, a way to work through fears, to reach a place of forgiveness, intimacy and unconditional love. The lessons can be many, and varied, but can be an opportunity for soul growth and a search for greater truth and awareness.

It is important to understand that dis-ease can manifest in many ways within the self. The result can be anger, fear, unhappiness, depression, etc., and all of these emotions can result in disease within the cells of the body. You are the only one who can bring ease into yourself. It is your actions and reactions which will allow for peace within. Honor yourself by taking responsibility for you. In doing so, life will be joyous and peaceful. And those around you will benefit from the energy you release into the universe.

Linda: I have repeatedly heard that "New Age" or New Thought thinkers do not take responsibility for their lives and, of course, I personally have found the opposite to be true.

Dr. Peebles: Yes. I would agree. If one embraces spiritual thought, then one understands that he is part of the God-essence, the Christ-love, and he cannot help but have self-responsibility. As God is the creator, so are each of you and that brings with it responsibility. When you take your life into your hands, then you hold the key. It is yours to do with as you want. You can stand in front of a locked door, put the key into your pocket and walk away. Or, you can place the key into the lock and turn it to see what awaits you on the other side of the door.

With metaphysical thought, comes insight that there is cause and effect in the universe. There is also change. The universe is ever-changing and each soul within the universe is changing. That is evolution. That is growth. That is truth.

The school Earth is a place of golden opportunity for growth. That is why you are there. It is a school of relationships. In order to have good relationships, one has to have a good relationship first with God and with self. Only then can other relationships have any value.

As you learn to incorporate the three principles into every day life, your struggles will lessen. You will see that the illusion of separation is just an illusion.

Linda: I know some will read this and become incensed by the idea that we create all that happens to us.

Dr. Peebles: Ah, yeah. You mean the bad things, the evil things such as being the victim of a heinous crime.

Linda: Yes. That is so difficult for most of us to understand that we might have had any part in creating that.

Dr. Peebles: Yes, it is a difficult concept to embrace. Now, if we can embrace the idea that we are here for lessons it might make it a little easier to accept. But if you remember that each of every one of you have illusions of separation, some greater than others, then you also know that everyone is on the same journey to re-discover love and intimacy and to let go of the fear of same.

Let's say you are mugged on the way home from work. You do not know your perpetrator and he does not know you. He has randomly picked you as his victim. Are you a victim in the sense that you created the event and refuse to take any responsibility for it? No. Are you the victim of his actions? Yes. But it will be what you do with this event in your life which will be of the greatest importance. Do you pace the streets with a gun in your hand looking to find this evil man so you can shoot him dead? Do you stay in your home, overcome with fear and afraid to step out your door? Do you curse every man you see who may look somewhat like the perpetrator? Do you fill every moment of your day with rage and anger? Or, do you increase your communication by encouraging some community effort to make your streets safer? If you choose the latter, then you have empowered yourself, you have become the creator—not the victim who remains paralyzed by the criminal act that was directed at you. You see?

Now, can you also understand the illusion of separation that this criminal carries within him? I am not saying that you need to forgive this person for his atrocious and vicious behavior, I am only saying that within your understanding of his fears, his need to dominate and over-power, you recognize a great illusion of separation. In understanding that, a part of you has come from a place of love for another human being on his journey, and a spark of forgiveness is there. So the first principle is in effect, and by reaching out to better your community in some way, you have achieved the other two principles, increased communication and self-responsibility.

No longer do you choose to be a victim. You have reclaimed your creativehood. You *are* the creator.

Linda: Can you explain a little about the difference between self-responsibility and selfishness?

Dr. Peebles: Do you mean how some acts of taking responsibility for self can be viewed by some as an act of selfishness?

Linda: Yes.

Dr. Peebles: Yeah. In order to come from a place of self-responsibility one has to come from the heart. In following the heart, it can never be judged as an act of selfishness. It can only be seen as loving allowance beginning with self. To be the creator, one has to take control of his life. If that means change, so be it. If ones lives his truth, then another cannot say that the man's truth is not his truth. Each of you have your own truth and to not live honestly by that truth is to live a lie, is it not?

Often, one man's truth is not another's. But by embracing the diversity, we allow for another's point of view, do we not?

If you relate this to relationships, then respect for the other's point of view is vital. If respect and allowance is absent then the relationship will falter, and in most cases, fail. If intimacy is embraced then you allow no barriers to stand in the way of honesty.

As long as respect is the focus then selfishness is not a part of one honoring thy self. Does that answer your question, Linda?

Linda: Yes, Dr. Peebles, thank you. Another thing I'd like to bring up about self-responsibility is the lack of responsibility in some people who do not allow or respect the diversity in others and inject their views of hate and intolerance into the public, whether it be via the media or the pulpit. They seem to have no idea, or even care, how their words will negatively affect people and would be the last to take any responsibility for playing a role in hate crimes or the like. Will you comment?

Dr. Peebles: Yes. Many couch their words in God's name. Their illusion of separation from their fellow-man is great. They cannot accept diversity of religion, sexual orientation, or politics, and in their fear, they lash out at those who are different from them in those ways.

Their intolerance is based on fear. Nothing else. Even though many of these individuals claim to have a close relationship with God, theirs is a relationship where God is separate, and the only way they can feel power is to speak out against those they believe not to be following God's laws. God's only law is love and the great master teacher from Nazareth, Jesus, spread the way of the law.

Now diversity will always be present and so will the illusion of separation. The only thing that will bring about new understanding is love. And that begins within your own heart. As love is put in motion, change can take place. As the three principles are used, a flicker of new understanding will result.

You are right that some do not seem to care what impact their bias and bigotry will have on others, but you must remember, different points of view have to be honored. And each person will at some time have to take responsibility for their actions, whether it be in this life time, or on the other side when they have a life review before them.

Also these lessons are lessons for all. When words of hate are given out, it has a two-sided effect. Some will agree and others will not. And it will be the ones who do not agree who will send out more love and understanding and it will grow. Love has the power to squelch hate.

So if one believes that he alone creates his life, all his experiences, his thoughts, his actions—and reactions—and takes full responsibility for that, then he can never be a victim. Fear, resentment, anger and hate fall away like the petals of a daisy caught up in the wind.

Love begets love. And love begins within self. The illusion of separation dissipates, intimacy prevails, and the creative force of self shines.

Linda: Dr. Peebles, you have said that Earth is a school of relationships. Why is it that so many have such problems keeping a loving relationship going and then when it ends there is so much anger and rage expressed, and love was what had originally brought them together?

Dr. Peebles: Yes. It is a school for relationships of every kind. Falling in love, loving another, can be an excellent example of an illusion. One may fall in love with only what they *expect* that person to be, not with *who* that person is. So it can be expectations and demands which become a part of the relationship, and sometimes an overpowering part. Is that really love? Not really. *I will love you if you change to the way I want you to be.* Love does not make any demands. It is allowing, respectful, and self-responsible. One does not have power over the other.

Throughout the years of a relationship, if both are not loving to the full extent of the meaning of the word, then fears build and respect is denied. Intimacy slowly leaves the relationship and as it does, fear of lack of same results. One may feel abandonment, rejection, and may soon look at themselves as a victim instead of looking at themselves as a willing participant, a creator. Remember, every thought, action and deed begins within and if one chooses not to take responsibility, then the blame falls to the other, does it not?

But, if one can take a careful look and recognize that he, or she, has created the deterioration of the relationship, for whatever reason, albeit varied life lessons, new avenues of growth, the desire for expanded experiences, and take responsibility for that, then the break in the relationship can come about without anger and resentment. It can be viewed as a time of growth, an opportunity for new understanding of self. Relationships never end, they just change. And change is part of growth.

Two people may be in a "loving" relationship to learn, and those lessons may be of only short endurance. Do not look at a broken relationship as a failure. For there are no failures, only growth.

As self-responsibility enters the picture, then the portrait takes on a new perspective. All strokes upon your canvas of life have special meaning. You are the artist, *always* the creator.

If one can break through the illusion of separation and diminish it, then one can understand that each is on their own unique journey and sometimes paths cross for only a short time in the scheme of things—but the crossing of paths will always have a place within the soul of each.

That is how growth occurs—by experiences. And each experience is as valid as the last, or the next.

Does that answer your question, Linda?

Linda: Yes, it does, but would you address the issue of spousal abuse which has become so prevalent in our society?

Dr. Peebles: Yes. With spousal abuse, or such, there are two victims. And often others—children—are victimized by being exposed to acts of violence within their home. To understand that there are two victims, the one who does the act of violence and the one who receives the violence, one has to recognize that *each* person involved is a victim because he or she does not take *self*-responsibility.

You see, when violence flares it is because of the illusion of separation. In this case, if it is the man who is violent, (and I must say, it usually is) he strikes out with mental or physical abuse because he has fear. He, of course, does not want anyone to think he is living in fear, and I must say that he goes to great lengths to hide his fear, but nonetheless, he has fear. Within himself he has a need to have power over the woman, to control her movement, her action, her response, and in some cases, becomes obsessed with that need. It is a search for intimacy, for acceptance, and within that search, and fear of same, he becomes desperate. In many cases, alcohol or drugs are in use which only lead to further distance from himself. So, in not accepting responsibility for his every action, he becomes caught up in victimhood. He fails to see that he has created the act by his own thoughts, actions and deeds. Because, for the moment, he does not have loving allowance for another or himself, nor does he have respect, and he has chosen to increase his communication in a violent way.

Now, the woman who is being victimized, is indeed a victim in every sense. But in allowing the behavior to continue more than once, she too, has not taken responsibility and continues to view herself as a victim. With loving allowance, always beginning with self, she needs to assure her safety, and in many cases the safety of her children. If she is caught up in her own fear of safety, fear of intimacy, and fear of the illusion of separation, then she may become immobilized. She may also believe that she *deserves* this kind of treatment. Often, with respect for self or for others absent from the relationship, she in some way, big or small, may be a party to the violence.

Now, if one or the other, or both, can examine the behavior within the relationship, and take self-responsibility, acknowledge that never are they a victim, always the creator, then change can take place. That change can come about through therapy, or by leaving the relationship.

Now it also has to be understood that one made a choice to have this kind of experience, if only for a moment. And if there will be other moments in the future is a decision to be made by self.

Violence is a signal that something is wrong within self. And change can only begin within. So do not look to the other person to change his ways, begin within your *self* and know that you are responsible for everything that you experience.

If the three principles are put in action and reaction, the resulting echo will bring about change.

Linda: This again shows how important the three principles are, Dr. Peebles. Can you speak of the energy dynamic of the principles—if there is one to be considered?

Dr. Peebles: Yeah. As we have said, thought is energy. And within the concept of the three principles is thought, which comes before action. So when one even begins to think of the three principles, energy is in motion and moves out and around and away from its source. Where does it go? Into the universe. It is no longer just a thought in the mind. It is a thing, a force and is alive and vibrant. And when the triad of principles are put in action and reaction, the force of that energy not only moves within the heart and mind of self, but radiates out touching all in its path. It spirals though the universe and gains momentum on its travel. The journey becomes one of gigantic proportion and is ever-expanding in energy. Because love is at its center, it radiates harmony and the spiraling energy becomes a fabric of eternity, never ending, never relenting in its power to bring about change.

Linda: Thank you, Dr. Peebles.

Dr. Peebles: God bless you, God bless you each and every one. Go your way in peace, love and harmony, for you are always the creator, never the victim. Hear my words, *always the creator*. Enjoy your journey through life. It is one of the greatest opportunities for growth. Do not take it all too seriously. Lighten up and enjoy the dance, as we enjoy dancing with you!

8

THE "ELUCIDATOR"

o o o o o o o o o o o o o o o o o o o o o o o o o o o o o o o o

"Enflower the pathway of humanity with the beautiful in life;
plant gardens of love in unhappy bosoms."

—*James Martin Peebles, 1869*

When pearls of wisdom become ours it matters little where they origi-
nated but many of us want to know *who* the teacher is.

It is for that reason I have presented James Martin Peebles to you.
We are looking only at a small slice of his life within these pages as his
earthly life was packed full of experiences, challenges and creativity in
those nearly one hundred years.

In reviewing his life, I would have to conclude that he was of genius
intelligence and greeted new ideas and philosophies with an open
mind. He had an apparent thirst for knowledge that was all-consuming
and had an ardent desire to share knowledge with others whether it be
with the pen or from the pulpit.

Whenever he lectured the hall would be filled with eager listeners,
and at times the listeners would number in the thousands. It was said
that he carried to the platform not only a strong individuality but a
personal presence which attracted and secured attention; was clear and
cutting as a speaker, yet poetic and sympathetic, emotional, hopeful
and confident.

As an author he was considered adept in massing his facts to carry conviction, was eloquent, keenly and sensitively perceptive, and his writings not only came from the heart, but reached out to the heart.

In 1858, a medium, entranced, gave him the appropriate title of the "Elucidator" because it was said that his "mission is to catch and elucidate thoughts, ideas and principles."

Around the turn of the last century, a young man, Archie Green, who had been Dr. Peebles' personal stenographer and typewriter, and who had worked for him in his San Diego sanitarium had this to say about Dr. Peebles in a biography by Professor Edward Whipple. The book, *A Biography of James M. Peebles, M.D., A.M.*, was written in 1901 when Dr. Peebles was close to eighty years of age.

"I beg to say that the Doctor is a genius with many striking peculiarities—a man out of the ordinary ruts of society. He has devoted, as you well know, a long life to the reforming and uplifting of his fellow men, and has oftentimes sacrificed much to make human hearts happier. He is so very sympathetic and kind-hearted that much of his time is occupied by strangers, calling to tell of their woes and sufferings, and to get his kindly advice and sympathy. No tramp goes from his door empty.

"Benevolence and generosity are among his strongest traits of character. These many times cause him to give to the unworthy. He is very easily imposed upon. He thinks everyone honest, judging them by himself. I never in my seven years of association with him, saw him angry nor heard him utter an unkind or profane word; but on the contrary, I have more than once seen him weep the tears of bitterness. He can hardly pass a child on the street without patting it on the head, and quite likely opening his purse, should it be decently filled. Children love and follow him. I have known him to give hundreds of dollars to the poor. But few know of these gifts. Only a few days since he took a family of poor children to a clothing store and in my presence supplied them with good winter clothing. He reads everything except novels. Sporting news he abominates. He is careless about his clothes, yet rigid in his diet. He often puzzles me. I would not care to come under his lance or scorching irony of his pen.

"The Doctor is a great lover of birds, flowers, music, trees, and children. He has quite often said if he could not find these in heaven he would return to earth where he could enjoy them. His paradise is a library. I have often known him to get up at midnight and write for hours.

"He is the most indifferent man to public opinion that I ever saw. I have traveled with him very much, and if he can start up a controversy on the cars with an orthodox preacher, he is happy. Some of the Seventh-day Adventists here think that the devil helps him. He has the Bible at his tongue's end, and I have heard him say that he and [Saint] Paul often differed. He will sometimes quote a passage, not in the Bible, and when told of it by an opponent, he will look up so innocently and say, 'Well, it ought to have been there.' At times he becomes so absorbed in thought while walking along the street that he will often go several blocks beyond his destination. When walking often I see him gesturing and talking to himself. Like others, he is a man of moods, and when in the mood of sadness, he flies to some old archaeological book, finding comfort in the accounts of the explorations of Egypt, Palestine, and Babylonia. He is naturally genial and social, and I believe him incapable of real anger, and yet he has several cannons concealed for those who attack his position in theology or medicine, or hygiene. He loathes fashion, calling it a tyrant, and I have sometimes thought he prided himself in going contrary to custom. At all events, he is always himself, and I am happy in being his private secretary."

Green's words seem to be in full agreement with the words of other friends and acquaintances of Dr. Peebles.

Mrs. H. F. M. Brown, a noted speaker and writer in the early history of Spiritualism, gave this description of Dr. Peebles in another biography, *The Spiritual Pilgrim*, by J. O. Barrett, published in 1872:

"Mr. Peebles's leading characteristic is, perhaps, *individuality*. He is independent in thought and speech; condemns cowardice and jealousies without stint: he commends where he can, never looking to see which way the tide is setting, or waits public approval. But he is quite willing that others should live their lives, if principles are not compromised. He is orderly, generous, social, mirthful, and a great lover of the beautiful.

"In personal appearance, he is tall, straight, of slender form, brown hair, blue eyes tending to hazel, his face is of Roman mold: his teeth faultless. He dresses with great care, avoiding alike the dandy and the sloven. He is tall and slim as a May-pole; as fair and frail as a delicate woman. Consumption looks him in the face occasionally; but, by sailing the world half round, he has eluded the unwelcome phantom. But, after all, the mistake might have been in putting the right soul into the wrong body. Spiritwise, Mr. Peebles is a mountaineer. He is calm in a storm, laughs at the lightning, and listens to the thunder as friend to friend. His thoughts, like mountain-streams, gush forth with freshness, music, and originality. If he is a thought-borrower, his benefactions are the ferns, the dewy mosses, the wild-flowers, the cloud-crowned hills, and green valleys of his native state. I said to my soul while listening to him, Emerson has this very man in his mind, when he said,—'In your heart are birds and sunshine: in your thoughts the brooklets flow.'"

The latter biographer, Edward Whipple, a long-time friend of Dr. Peebles, spent time in Dr. Peebles' home while preparing his book. Whipple wrote, "He [Dr. Peebles] has lived in strict accordance with the text embraced in the following three words: temperance, industry, fraternity. His diet, his exercise, his cleanliness in both body and soul, his conversation, and his general habits through life have been ordered in accordance with the laws of temperance. All his waking hours are employed in a manner to serve a given end; and it is because they have been so employed that his years have been blessed with such productive and magnificent results. Moreover, he has always kept in close touch with the great heart of our common humanity, advocating both popular and unpopular reforms. In all races, and kindreds, and tongues, he sees a common bond of fellowship, a bond far too close and fraternal to

suit the feelings of certain exclusives, who cherish an inveterate prejudice against all people not included in their own ethnic classification.
This sentiment of universality, this feeling of fraternity endears our
brother to the common people, and makes him a citizen of the world.

"When at home, the Doctor retires between eight and nine o'clock,
P. M., sleeps well, and rises early,—always before the sun appears
above the brown crest of Mount San Miguel. He may be seen any
morning as soon as it is light, walking bareheaded, and often bare-
footed, in his garden—in a veritable paradise of roses—going from
cluster to cluster, tenderly caressing the responsive petals, and taking in
their rich aromas. He knows his flowers well, and they behave as
though they knew and loved him, and were anxious to impart to him
their wealth of aromal essence for the replenishment of that vital and
magnetic abundance, which so habitually belongs to his personal
sphere.

"He makes no use of stimulants, not even coffee or tea. He rarely
touches animal food,—pork, never,—but his table is amply provided
with various cereals, nuts, vegetables, fruits, honey, milk, cheese, but-
ter, etc. His dress is uniformly of broadcloth, but he is in no sense dud-
ish or foppish. He abhors the current fashions....

"His magnetic presence and perennial cheerfulness diffuses a perpet-
ual joy and sunshine throughout the whole house. His conversation,
though often racy, pungent, and abounding in witticisms, is chaste and
refined. Intimate with him for over thirty years, we never heard a
coarse or vulgar expression fall from his lips.

"Dr. Peebles is a good illustration of one of the titles to his various
books, 'How to Live a Century and Grow Old Gracefully.' Though
eighty years of age in a few months, the lines in his face are soft and full
of youthful expression. His step is airy and light. His frame is well filled
out, so that he is both portly and tall. He is still projecting labors which
it would seem would demand a lifetime to carry out, while there
appears to be no abatement in his mental productiveness. His study
may be compared to a field in preparation for a new crop, full of poten-

tial possibilities, but the crop in prospect does not present a very attractive appearance to the eye,—books, papers, scraps, and unfinished manuscripts lying all about. For the most part, he stands at his desk while writing, but much of his literary composition is dictated to an amanuensis,—dictated rapidly, as he alternately walks the floor or sits in a rocking chair. While thus engaged, witticisms frequently burst forth as a by-play which serves to 'oil the hinges of the mind' and keeps the mental machinery in easy motion. In discussion, the Doctor often seems scathing, bitter, and biting; but beneath the biting there's a spirit of love and fraternity. The words are severe, but the heart is tender and true. The hand that lifts the axe holds the balm to heal the wound."

Professor Whipple stated that Dr. Peebles possessed acute intuition, and was decidedly optimistic in his philosophy of life. He also expressed that Dr. Peebles spoke and wrote in intelligible language, directly to the hearts and minds of people, and that he was eloquent, bold, reckless, and daring, and at the same time, sensitive, impressible, and reticent. Dr. Peebles' life had been spent in the midst of the moving throngs, in close contact with the populace and had always been immensely popular.

Whipple scribes, "Gifted with a fine presence and a fluent eloquence, his acquaintance has been widely sought, his society courted, his literary productions widely circulated, while tens of thousands have been attracted and charmed by his public ministrations. He is almost as well known in the Orient as in the Occident. Thousands have flocked to hear his lectures in England, New Zealand, Australia, India, Ceylon, and China. In our own country his public utterances have been listened to in almost every town and hamlet."

During his remaining years following the publication of the second biography, Dr. Peebles not only continued his world travels, but authored several more books and was active almost to the very end of his life.

In the summer of 1990, a few days before *To Dance With Angels* was released, I came across a newspaper article from 1920 which mentioned Dr. Peebles' book, *How to Live a Century and Grow Old Gracefully*. When Don and I read the article, and were in discussion about it, it dawned on each of us at about the same moment, that we had written our original manuscript in approximately the number of days that had remained following Dr. Peebles' death on February 15, 1922, and what would have been his one hundredth birthday, March 23, 1922. We both broke out in copious goose bumps and shivers as we realized that we had allowed, through the writing of our book, for Dr. Peebles to reach the century mark with his words.

Dr. Peebles, on the occasion of his ninety-eighth birthday, speaking to the Octogenarian and Centenarian Clubs in California, had this to say of longevity: "I am safely embarked at the present time on my ninety-ninth yearly voyage across the tempestuous ocean of human life.

"Often I am asked, 'How have you lived so long in this struggling and tiresome world?' Negatively, I have lived in ease and idleness, nor have I lived to sensually fatten on human flesh, animal food, or various stimulants.

"'But what are the general causes of your nearing a century of years?' Many are the reasons. In the first place I was born of healthy yet poor parents in the pure, bracing air of mountainous Vermont. Becoming in middle life, a practicing physician, I feel to deliberately say that, breathing being the first thing in life and the last thing at death, it is natural and necessary that we breathe pure air by day and also by night. The next reason is light; light is an inspiring and vitalizing force, and sunshine is ever a strong and powerful invigorator.

"Be as wise as the birds and flocks in the field—retiring early at night and rising with the morning sun—is sound common sense. Dress loosely....White is much healthier clothing than black. Sandals are healthier than shoes. Eating animal flesh is both expensive and morally injurious to the higher nature.

"This astounding twentieth century not only pleadingly invites, but persistently demands seer and sages—demands plain and brave talk, clean habits, righteous purposes, and a rigid practice of all the ennobling, uplifting principles that tend to promote long life, brotherhood and the redemption of a world-wide humanity.

"Old age in a rightly lived life is rich and golden in meditation. I would sooner be 98 than 48.

"Sick of the city's tumult, and the world's selfish strife, I sometimes ask: 'Is there no sunny nook in this great Father-Mother universe, where books, birds, flowers and the music of ever-flowing streams tell and sing of quietness and peace? Is there no tropic isle in southern seas, far away from the world's traffics, suspicious, competitions and crushing jealousies, where loving hearts blend like rainbow hue—blend as do the joys of angels and the fadeless loves of the gods?'

"Upon the whole, this is a beautiful world, being God's world. Five times have I circled it. The incense of Oriental gardens still clings to my garments and the solemn music of the historic Nile still murmurs in my memory. Spices never lose their perfumes. Good thoughts never die. Modern science and psychic research—God's right and left-hand angels—have demonstrated the continuity of life. Death is simply a disguised deliverance, or, like the budding rose, it climbs up on the garden wall to bloom on the other side.

"Inspiration is universal. It over-swept with grandeur all the past ages, and is just as fresh now as in time's earliest morning. Poets, as much as prophets, are illumined with a divine radiance. They think, they write and sing from the very depths of their being.

"Aged, very aged in years, I am; soon can I say with Tennyson—'I go to prove my soul, I see my way as birds see their trackless way, I shall arrive.'"

◆   ◆   ◆

Most mediums who channel Dr. Peebles, and the recipients of his spiritual teachings via these mediums, know little of his earthly life, partly because the Doctor does not offer a lot of information about his time on Earth, and partly because biographical information is not easy to come by.

Several years ago I had asked Dr. Peebles how many channels he was then working with and coming through.

His answer: "Ah, well, let's keep it in North America for now. That will keep it simple. I work around the world through various channels and in North America, let's see, there are twenty-five different channels I come through. There are others who are stretching for my presence and those that I work with and represent, and that's wonderful, but there's some more stretching to do before becoming effective channels."

He also told Don and I that he finds a somewhat different experience through each channel. With some channels he can bring through more scientific information and language, or more of the feminine aspect, or sexuality, and through some, only a *part* of him comes through effectively.

I personally know several people who channel Dr. Peebles, several in trance-state, others in a similar way that I do, through clairaudience or clairvoyance. But with each, there is no doubt that Dr. Peebles is communicating. There is a recognizable rhythm, a resonance, that belongs only to him.

In late 1990, we received a letter from an elderly man in the Mid-West who, beginning in the late 1940's, had often experienced Dr. Peebles through various Spiritualist mediums. I followed up on that by contacting one of the country's leading Spiritualist communities and it was affirmed for me that Dr. Peebles often came through some of their Spiritualist mediums, although the woman was a little reluctant to offer that information and it was understandable that she wanted to protect the religious sanctity of the event.

Trance-mediumship is hard work and all-consuming. Thomas Jacobson, who was our first link-up to the grand spirit, retired from mediumship a few years ago, after working with Dr. Peebles for about fifteen years.

Many, many years ago, in 1869 to be precise, Dr. Peebles penned: "Live to lift up others, to brighten the chain of friendship, to educate the mind and heart for a heaven on earth."

Obviously, now in spirit, he still holds dear that same philosophy.

For me, as it was for Don, our contact with Dr. Peebles serves to further validate that consciousness and personality survives the death of the body.

Dr. Peebles, now residing in the spirit world, still possesses his earthly personality and all the wisdom which he had so bountifully accumulated while on Earth. One cannot help but think that this man's life journey came about as close to what is considered enlightenment as one could come. Now from the other side, he has even further expanded his wisdom and understandings. His spiritual communication is always laced with wit and wisdom, compassion and love for humanity.

We are lucky to be recipients of his love and wisdom as his mission continues.

9

THE ECHO

○ ○
"Life is a joy, especially as you surrender to the delightful opportunities for growth, each and every day."

—The grand spirit, Dr. Peebles

I have discovered that there is something of a common effect which is shared by all who experience the loving touch of Dr. Peebles, whether that contact is direct or through the written word, and it matters not one's social status, age, sex, educational background, or religious propensity. Although each human being on this planet is absolutely unique, and in turn his or her encounter with Dr. Peebles is unique—a commonality of impression takes place. In addition, one often finds that even while Dr. Peebles is sharing his spiritual psychology with another person regarding that person's unique situation, his words can be of benefit to everyone who hears or reads them.

For that reason, within these chapters I will be sharing with you a selection of personal testaments which I hope will strike a chord within many of you. By examining the impact that the teachings of Dr. Peebles has had on others, and how those teachings have been incorporated into daily lives, it may inspire and enable you to put them into use in your own life.

The most typical effects that Dr. Peebles has had on people are: He touched my heart and soul; his words resonated throughout my entire body; I was moved in a deeply profound way; I felt such love, joy, and peace; my life will be forever changed; and on and on.

It has often been reported that the effect of Dr. Peebles' words have been electric.

An eminent and widely respected psychiatrist, the late Paul S. Weisberg, M.D., was one who was affected in that way. In 1987, Dr. Weisberg, after being told by Dr. Peebles that he was about at the end of his cycle of lives, had asked what he would do when that was done. According to Dr. Weisberg, the grand spirit's reply was, "You'll probably come up and be like me; you have this love of Earth and love of humanity, and you'll come up and help people. Even now you are a guide when you're between lives."

Dr. Weisberg told us, "The effect of his words on me was activating, like an electric charge."

Dr. Weisberg stated that several of his patients had spoken to Dr. Peebles on his referral and that each had "marvelous experiences with him."

Not long after, Dr. Weisberg, a past president of the American Society of Adolescent Psychiatry and one of the pioneers in group therapy, moved his highly successful private practice from Washington. D.C. to Beverly Hills, California, to enable him to work closer with Dr. Peebles and Jacobson.

Paul Weisberg died in 1989. But that is not the end of the story.

In October of 1990, two months after our book, *To Dance With Angels* was published, a letter was received from a woman who lived in the West. I will quote a portion of that letter:

> "...when I was in my early twenties, I am now thirty-nine, I was seeing a psychiatrist in Washington D.C. named Paul Weisberg. A few weeks ago I woke up thinking about him a lot, that morning in an elevator I saw someone who really reminded me of him. A little while later, I went into a book store, walked directly to the back of the store and grabbed the book [*To Dance With Angels*]. When I opened it and saw the dedication to Paul S. Weisberg I felt so

strange. I felt like I had been pushed into the store, I never go to the New Age Psychology sections, I am a poetry, garden and cook-book type of person, nor was it a visible selection. I did not buy the book then, I was too spooked. However, I since have bought the book recognizing that I was 'guided' to it (I even feel silly using that word). I am now reading the book, but I'm frightened, not by what I read, just sort of scared I'm going to read something so directed at myself. It's so supernatural. Can you tell me why this happened to me?...."

I immediately telephoned the woman to give her some reassurance. She informed me that she had been feeling a little troubled before she came upon the book. And that first day in the book store she was so shocked when the first thing she saw was our dedication to Dr. Weis-berg. She had left the store in tears. She also said that when she had bought the book, returned home, randomly opened it, what she read on that page had to do with her past issues which had again come up for her in recent days. By the end of our conversation, I believe I had calmed her fears and given her reassurance that her psychiatrist was still on the job!

There is a specialness about Dr. Peebles which is so difficult to put into words. It appears that once you encounter him, he is always at your side. And for many, the encounter can be life-changing.

I'm sure Lee Chaifetz will attest to that. In July of 1988, Lee was diagnosed with leukemia. The guidance he was given by Dr. Peebles was beneficial and gave Lee insight into his disease, and hope, which he much needed, that his life would continue.

Lee's wife at that time, Carol, went to a public gathering being held by Thomas Jacobson and Dr. Peebles on the night following Lee's sec-ond day in the hospital. She was distressed as would be expected as she asked Dr. Peebles about her husband's condition. Those of us who knew and loved Lee listened in dismay to Carol's question to the Doc. Here is that exchange:

> *Carol: Hi, Dr. Peebles, this is Carol.*
>
> *Dr. Peebles: Hi, Carol. God bless you, my dear.*
>
> *Carol: God bless you too. My husband, Lee, who I know you know, was admitted to the hospital yesterday and the doctors say that he has one of the forms of leukemia and so…well, what we're wanting to know…it seems—I don't know, maybe we're wrong, it seems like it is pretty bad, but we haven't gotten all of the results back. We want to know what the source is, what the lesson is to be learned, and what we need to do. And by what we need to do, I mean do we go with the medical treatments, do we go to a holistic healer or…I guess we'd really like to know if this is his time—and, you know…so we'll know how to deal with it.*

I can't even begin to describe the silent tension which was in that room that night as we all waited to hear Dr. Peebles' response.

Lee was to later admit, "As I lay in the hospital, I felt confused but still curious about what Dr. Peebles could tell me about my situation."

Here is the message that came forward that night for Lee from Dr. Peebles:

"Lee, you are a beautiful soul and you are a great soul. Part of you understands this and part of you disbelieves the same. For you have a great fear of responsibility. I speak not of the day-to-day affairs of mankind, but fear of responsibility in applying your own self—intimacy, Lee, between you and the world around you.

"You are—as a soul, as a spirit—in frequent discussion with us over here in the past year or so. And in this discussion you have understood greater clarity of anger, anger within your own being directed at your self, feeling and believing that you have wasted so much time, and disbelieving that you can, in the body, truly love your intimacy, creativity, through your own power.

"You are then in fear of total application in this present life. Part of you wants to leave and start over again, not as an escape but out of fear that you are repeating old errors and that it would be better to end this present dance with your karma and try again in a different body.

"However, your work as a spirit is far from over in this lifetime, my friend. Yes, this particular disease has some hold inside of you. I would suggest that this hold is somewhat firm and that this disease is responding to your own requests and requirements, Lee. You will find that the days, the weeks, and months ahead will be the most powerful, meaningful, and beautiful of your entire present lifetime. Reflection, reevaluation, life decisions—your healing in the body with leukemia is related to a series of decisions—decisions of your adamant, firm, unqualified commitment to presence of your own creative soul, the child within.

"To love responsibility, thereby the echo—the echo of the world you fear, and have such frustration of—from your past, Lee—this is your work and this will be your greatest prayer meditation of all, this disease at hand.

"This is not a passing condition, Lee. This is deep within you, and it's going to take some great prayer on your part—and you are going to manifest this prayer—for your plan is to stay in the body, not to leave the body yet.

"However, you will have to work hard and prove to yourself—not to anyone else—your commitment to absolute presence. So we encourage you to go forward with treatment through traditional medical practices, and as well you seek out a holistic healer who understands energy fields, manipulation, and movement of those electromagnetic fields of your self—such as a very skilled acupuncturist, for example, and acquire treatment there as well."

Lee was given additional instruction in specific meditation procedures including making friends with the living forces of leukemia. Dr. Peebles assured Lee that the meditations would give him "an entirely new excitement about life."

Seven months later, Lee had this to say, "While the doctors spoke of symptoms and percentages, Dr. Peebles addressed my habits and attitudes. Considering my circumstances, I decided there was no reason why I couldn't incorporate all the advice I was being given, both medical and spiritual. I agreed to my doctor's suggestions for treatment and followed Dr. Peebles suggestions of a schedule of meditations and additional holistic treatment [acupuncture].

"Taking the advice of Dr. Peebles and my acupuncturist, I have adjusted my eating habits. I have made some definite changes in my style of communicating with others. I have given up much of my anger and fear, and can feel the world moving toward me more than ever before.

"As of this writing, seven months after my diagnosis, my doctor informs me that my blood profile is completely normal, and if I were not to tell a physician examining me about my condition and treatment, he would be hard pressed to diagnose my illness correctly.

"Because of the success of my own physical health, I have much gratitude and no doubts about the insights I have gained through contact with Spirit, and if my faith in our eternal nature had not been renewed by contact with Dr. Peebles, I wonder where I might be right now."

◆   ◆   ◆

But Lee's battle was not over. His leukemia did have a firm hold on him as Dr. Peebles had indicated and it was not yet ready to give up that hold, nor apparently was Lee. In November of 1997, nearly nine and a half years following his diagnosis, Lee shares the events which followed:

"In February of 1989, I was following Dr. Peebles' advice and my health had stabilized. I now realize, that my reluctance to follow through as the year went by, led to my cancer becoming acute. In a private session, Dr. Peebles informed me that this need for my soul to learn self-responsibility had led me to the present situation. I had explored many alternative therapies, some incredibly effective, some not at all. By the end of the year, time had run out. To *not* have a transplant meant death.

"In February of 1990 I had a bone marrow transplant at the City of Hope in Duarte, California. It is an incredible monument to scientific healing. My type of cancer was chronic myelogenous leukemia. My provider, Dr. Pablo Parker, a remarkable man, was completely aware of my beliefs and would allow me to incorporate any healing that didn't openly conflict with his scheduled plan of treatment. If I would fail a blood pressure test, he would allow me to meditate, and take the test again, before prescribing further medicine.

"By being able to donate his marrow to me, my brother Lenny was proud, but incredibly modest. Given a chance to save my life, he never hesitated for a moment. The whole event drew us much closer together to this day.

"My physical recovery from the chemotherapy, radiation and various blends of medicines is still on going. During the past seven years, I was hospitalized multiple times. I have had infections, pneumonia, paralysis, multiple surgeries, and just about every medical test and drug there is. I have had both lenses in my eyes replaced due to cataracts, nerve damage in my legs, and last December, had my left knee joint replaced.

"I mention all these because despite the fantastic medical care I received, I believe the real reason for my survival and gradual recovery, has been my ability to address the issues that Dr. Peebles spoke to me about back in July of 1988.

"This is what enabled me to play golf three times last week."

◆   ◆   ◆

You have just read how Dr. Peebles influenced Lee at a very critical time in his life and his dramatic story sure can make one believe in miracles. As we all know, not everyone in need of a bone marrow transplant is even lucky enough to find a compatible donor. The procedure is an extreme one. All defenses of the body are destroyed as drugs tear down the immune system in preparation for a foreign substance, someone else's bone marrow, to find its place within the body and bring it back to a healthy state. And sometimes it fails to achieve that goal.

As you can see in Lee's case, it can be a rough struggle back as the chemotherapy and heavy drugs which are a necessary bombardment to the body can also do some damage.

But on that July night in 1988, most wondered if Lee would even be able to release the firm hold those leukemia cells had on him. I know we all prayed he could.

Lee had been "instructed" by Dr. Peebles on how to receive the gift of bone marrow from his brother. While marrow was harvested from Lenny's hip, in another wing of the hospital, Lee prepared his state of mind and body to receive the gift of life.

Lee reports, "It was time for me to accept the world around me, the true issue of my disease. The moment had come when I could no longer survive alone. Without my brother's gift, my life was over."

As the healthy life-giving substance began its journey down the intravenous tubing into the catheter which had been surgically inserted near his left collarbone, Lee concentrated on his desire to live by welcoming the marrow and acknowledging that he was ready to begin a new life.

Miracles do happen—whether guided by spirit or influenced by our own soul-strength—God can find a way to bring about a miracle.

I have known for quite some time that Lee uses what he calls "the trinity of the three principles" in his professional business life as well as his personal. I asked Lee to share with us how he has put the principles to use in the business world. Now, more than ten years after he first encountered Dr. Peebles and his principles, Lee has this to say:

"It is no coincidence, that each time I've seen, heard or communicated with Dr. Peebles, he has reminded me that Earth is a school and the only curriculum that will enable us to graduate is:

-loving allowance, starting with yourself
-increased communication with respect
-self-responsibility.

"Only all three, in combination, will take us where our souls long to be. To deny any one of the three is to inhibit the power of the process.

"At first, these ideas were simply philosophical fancies that attracted my attention. The thing that impressed me was the way that Dr. Peebles would use one or another of the principles to lead so many different people to awareness of their power and abilities, no matter how desperate their situations. Each time, they would begin frustrated and confused and at the end of each encounter, they would be relaxed, informed and empowered.

"I began to employ these three principles in my own personal life as best I could. And failed miserably on many occasions. Yet I began to see that the blueprint of these three concepts, when applied to any relationship or event, would yield amazing joy, creativity and productivity. To me, they are the simplest cure for the human condition.

"For almost twenty years, I have earned my living in sales. A few years ago, I was given the opportunity to become sales manager. I had known the owners a long time, and was trained by them. I was, therefore, given complete free reign in style. Since this was new territory, I had to make choices about policy and goals. I knew these choices would determine the success or failure of the department down the road.

"An inner voice whispered to me, *'Why not just use the three principles in each individual situation and see what happens?'*

"This was the beginning of enormous growth and profit for the company. My sales force more than doubled in two years and the profits, and the improvements in the lives of the work force along with them.

"In a sense, all these ideas are a stopwatch, that enables us to accept others as different, for a moment. To learn that only by connecting with our fellow humans, and by taking responsibility in our own lives, can we realize that earth is one of many heavens."

◆   ◆   ◆

Nita Reynolds Trocosso underwent a tranformational recovery after years of depression, despair, and endless rounds of therapy following her encounter with the grand spirit psychologist, Dr. Peebles more than ten years ago. Nita stated at that time, "There are those rare moments when an extraordinary event or person is instrumental in changing the course forever of one's life. For me that was Dr. Peebles."

I asked Nita to give my readers her thoughts on what influence the three principles have had on her life since Dr. Peebles facilitated her road to recovery. This is what Nita wanted to share:

"To put it simply I would have to say that the greatest impact upon my life has been in my personal relationships and with my children. The three principles always give me a place to go and a place to rest, all the while allowing me to take one hundred percent responsibility, to surrender and be in control at the same time. This is a comfort and strength that I would have called an impossible contradiction many years ago.

"Loving allowance helps me to accept myself and all those parts I had worked for years to rid myself of. Increased communication continues to teach me the value of listening, the gift of compassion, and has restored laughter to me. And self-responsibility is in my face, not letting me get away with blaming others and though painful at times, its other side continues to remind me that I have the power to change the way I *think and feel* and I am the master of my destiny.

"It is this sense of freedom that I sought my whole life and most of the time, now, I do feel free. My life has been so incredibly altered. I went from feeling separate and alone most of the time to feeling one hundred percent of the time connected to God and the spirit that guides me. About ninety-eight percent of the time I feel connected to those around me as well as to strangers I meet and even to ants marching down my sidewalk.

"I no longer live my life with regrets. I'm clear about my priorities and I no longer think about what my future will be. For me, that is something. I am now comfortable with *me*—and that is about the biggest biggy of my life."

"I find it difficult to explain the eternal quality that the three principles possess and how they evolve as I do. They have become more worthwhile in my life as I grow. Timeless wisdom is such a challenge to articulate."

Nita's life overflows with enthusiasm and creativity. As a gifted art teacher, she inspires her young students to grow, expand and revel in their own creativity. Dr. Peebles' influence allowed Nita to find herself. He not only gave a gift to Nita by giving her insight and enabling her to heal, but he gave us all a gift. Just ask the children in her art classes, they will tell you.

◆　　◆　　◆

Timeless wisdom can be difficult to articulate or to even fully understand unless your life has been personally changed as a result of taking in some of that wisdom. Jery Dickinson is another who feels that Dr. Peebles and his spiritual guidance has changed her life. When I met her recently, I found her to be self-assured, outgoing and enthusiastic. I didn't have a clue as to her previous fear of intimacy. But she has graciously agreed to share some of her struggles with us.

In Jery's own words: "What I wanted the most and what I feared the most were practically one in the same thing. I desperately wanted to love and be loved, but I came into this life convinced that pain must be avoided at all costs, and had a paralyzing fear of vulnerability and rejection. I avoided conflicts in order to avoid being seen as less than perfect…undesirable as a friend or lover. I manipulated people and relationships to prevent anyone from getting close. I had a predisposition for self-recrimination. I no longer had the ability to experience emotion. I had a lifetime of rejections and various abuses to support my belief that I was a victim. That's the sorry state I was in when I met Dr. Peebles. He very patiently explained his three principles to me, but at the time, I didn't fully understand that they were the key to going down the road that I so desperately wanted to travel.

"The first thing I did was actually the last thing I came to understand. I created an experience, a doorway so to speak, to provide the opportunity to learn. The experience itself isn't what's of importance…having allowed it was the giant leap forward. Toward the end of the situation I said to Dr. Peebles, 'I made myself extremely vulnerable to this man. I engaged in conflict in an effort to resolve our old issues, even though it was terribly difficult for me. I showed him more of myself than I've ever shown anyone, yet in the end, I was still rejected. I know there's a point here…what am I missing?' He chuckled and exclaimed, '…and you didn't die from it did you!' He was right. I didn't die. What I had done during this two year process was come to life in ways I would have never dreamed possible.

"I realized things that are now, thankfully, a part of me, and in my quiet moments I review my day to see if I used every opportunity to practice what I've been taught. The knowledge and understanding that there is no rejection, merely different points of view, which I must honor and respect as much as I would my own, has freed me from my fears. My pain of the past came from my resistance to change and any pain in the future will be a signal to me to look for the source of my resistance.

"I shed centuries of guilt, finally realizing that I'm not perfect and never will be. God doesn't expect that from me, or anyone, why should I?

"I can, and do, make myself vulnerable…show myself…and in doing so make it possible for others to respond to me in kind. I communicate with less and less reservation who I am, where I've been, the baggage I've carried and what I think and feel; more often than not, while laughing at myself. The response from those around me, as well as from within myself, never ceases to be a source of amazement. At this point, I'm sure Dr. Peebles is looking over my shoulder saying, 'Well, didn't we tell you so!'

"I'm now capable of emotion. The first experience was tears, unexpected and startling, because there seemed to be no apparent reason for them. I was moved…touched, and I can't begin to explain the joy I felt. I've joined the human race! I'm alive and finally allowing life to touch me. I now let emotion sweep over me whenever and wherever, and make no apologies, because this ability to feel is one of the most wonderful gifts I've ever given myself.

"I came to a point where there was an acceptance, a knowing, that these principles would be a major part of my life, and as I grow and expand, my awareness of how they can be applied will grow and expand with me.

"I get up in the morning looking forward to life, and whatever mystery and adventure it may hold. I no longer greet the day angry and depressed at the thought of, yet another day, as the victim I used to perceive myself to be."

Life-changing? You tell me.

◆   ◆   ◆

I believe it takes special people to become hospice caregivers. Marie McDaniel is one of those special people. She has done hospice care for a couple of years and she says it is her way of putting one of Dr. Peebles' principles to work in her life.

When I interviewed Marie, a mother of three grown children, I was most interested in how Dr. Peebles had influenced her decision to become a hospice caregiver. This is what she had to say:

"Dr. Peebles' philosophy and his three principles have had an overwhelming impact on my life. The principles are simple and basic things you can go by as you move along your life's path. They teach love. How can you go wrong with that one? And it starts with self-love. You can't find anything negative about this. It is a natural belief system instead of the regiment of a bunch of rules and regulations. It is a natural love thing. It is self-responsibility. His philosophy does not preach, it teaches love.

"I knew I needed to increase my communication, that's something I personally had a problem with, so I decided one way to apply the principle and increase my communication was to get out there and do hospice work.

"I have always had a good philosophy on death, myself, but Dr. Peebles has verified my peacefulness with death. I then knew my belief was really okay, I was not a nut, or in denial about death. He is such an old person and lived here long before I was born and the philosophy still holds true. So he verified my personal belief."

I asked Marie if her fuller understanding of death, and life after death, has made hospice work more desirable for her and if it has brought something into her hospice caregiving.

She replied, "Yes, it truly has. I guess there's not that panic that a lot of people feel while watching someone go through the end of life. It's a sense of ease. Now I can watch them leave with ease and not feel I have to try and hold them here. It's really okay for them to go and do this thing, this metamorphose to the other side.

"In hospice work you are not allowed to really discuss your philosophy that much but it is amazing how my patients end up expressing and believing the same things I do, and it doesn't seem to matter whether they are Catholics, Jewish, or whatever their religious background. At the very end, they all kind of ease out of it. I've not seen panic. They find a place of peace. I think it is just something that comes natural…I hope. But from what I've seen so far, it does."

Marie is a warm, compassionate person, and I know her presence at the bedside of a dying patient has to help one to find that "ease." And I'm sure her loving support of the grieving family is very special and helps them through a very difficult time.

Marie has also served as a midwife on several occasions over the years which has given her the opportunity to assist in birth into a new world. Now, with hospice, she again helps with a new birth into a world we all know as home.

In the words of the grand spirit, "There is no death; there is only change."

Nearly a hundred and twenty years ago, James Martin Peebles stated, "In the divine light of present inspirations and spiritual revelations there is no death,—only incarnations, changes, and ceaseless successions of births."

Marie is right. Dr. Peebles had a broad understanding of death while he was here in the body and he has carried that forward with him to the world of spirit. And now, while in the spirit world, he knows the absolute truth which he delights in sharing with us. We do not die when our physical body is shed.

He had often written, "There is no death!" In his book, *Immortality,* he wrote, "Seen in the light of the spiritual philosophy, and studied from the Mount of Vision, death is but a hyphen connecting the two worlds—is but a renunciation of the physical body—is but a flower-wreathed arch under which mortals march on one by one to the shining shores of immortality; or it may be compared to the rosebud that climbs up the shaded garden-wall to bloom on the sunward side."

He also penned, "When born I died and when I die I shall be born....As the physical birth of the infant is death to the placenta-envelope, so birth into spirit-life involves the death and disintegration of the physical casket. And while this latter process is as natural as beautiful, it implies no disorganization of the spiritual body—no cessation of conscious existence. Duality of being extends to human consciousness. The *inner* consciousness—related to the Infinite Consciousness of the universe, God—is never for a moment suspended. And just prior to, and during the change called dying, it often flames up the brightest."

10

OVERCOMING THE ILLUSIONS

o o o o o o o o o o o o o o o o o o o o o o o o o o o o o o o o
"You are the paintbrush, life is the canvas. Learn this, and you will never feel the victim again."

—*The grand spirit, Dr. Peebles*

Dr. Peebles often reminds us that one of our greatest challenges, and in turn, our greatest pain, can come from relationships, especially those relationships with the ones closest to us.

We literally create our own reality by the way we choose to perceive our inner and outer world. The harder we try to manipulate and control our reality, the more we interfere with the universe's ability to give us what we want. It takes energy to manipulate and control and to worry. Our thoughts take on energy, become real, become matter. I'm sure most of us have spent sleepless hours when our thoughts are focused on a problem in our lives. Instead of awakening refreshed, we begin our day exhausted, and our problem is still as evident as it was, still unresolved. Instead of energizing our body with rest, we have unnecessarily used up energy by worrying. Much worry and stress can be eliminated from our lives if we can only learn to put our problems in the hands of a higher power. By letting go, and letting God, it puts into motion a movement toward a solution. Our mind becomes uncluttered, unstressed, and when possible solutions present themselves we are able to see much more clearly.

If we awaken each new day with enthusiasm and joy instead of with an apprehension that the world will *attack* us today, will not our inner world be more peaceful and harmonious? Do we fear our world and consider it to be filled with uncertainty or do we embrace it with excitement and consider it to be filled with delicious mysteries? Do we feel that happiness is not ours, or do we acknowledge that happiness is a state of mind? Our mind.

Are we prepared to disavow victimhood and acknowledge that we are empowered to create our world to our choosing? Reality is our creation and when we are able to acknowledge and accept that to its fullest, not only do we become free, but it enables us to be the best we can be.

If we put loving allowance into action, beginning with self, then we reclaim our unique worth, we become convinced that we are not failures, or sinners, and that we are here on Earth in human form to learn how our unique differences contribute to a perfect whole in the spiritual unity. In doing this, we recognize that God loves us *exactly* the way we are.

Dr. Peebles often brings it to our attention that only a subtle movement of the soul marks the difference between a saintly act and a murderous act. Both are motivated by the same desire for acceptance and love although one is expressed positively and the other negatively. But both are a movement toward God, *because all movements in the universe are God moving upon Himself,* and no other movements are possible.

So from this point of view, then, there are no saints, and no murderers, per se, no failure, no error, no sin, no death; all movements of the soul are growth and all paths lead to God.

If we come to understand that we all share a common bond, a common purpose, then how can we not have compassion for one another?—how can we not support one another? We need to stop condemning, stop warring, stop hating, stop isolating. If we can start loving, make that our conscious goal, then maybe we can discover God at the center of *us*.

What seems to be apparent in love relationships of the opposite sex is not only the illusion of separation which we all have to deal with but the social and cultural dynamics which come into play. I used to be one to argue that men and women were not different. I no longer give that argument because I now believe that there are basic innate and cultural disparities, especially in the way we relate and communicate with one another. Women are nurturers by nature. Men are protectors. With each of these roles, can be the need to control. And at times, those roles, interacting upon each other, result in misunderstanding and conflict—leading to a greater illusion of separation, loss of intimacy, and often, a breakdown of the relationship.

But by putting Dr. Peebles' principles into action within a relationship, the relationship can be made stronger and more enduring.

I'm sure Dr. Peebles can give us insight into successful love relationships. We will see what he has to say.

Linda: Hello, Dr. Peebles. As we have discussed, one of the most difficult relationships that people have is the love relationship. The soaring divorce rate in this country is a good example of the difficulty in keeping love intact. Could you give some additional insight into that.

Dr. Peebles: God bless you. Yes, Linda, we would be happy to. When one brings fear of intimacy forward in a relationship it takes work to break through that fear. The fear of intimacy can be based on many of life's earlier experiences, in addition to the experiences of many life times of the past. And within this life time, past experiences build up in the conscious and subconscious mind. In other words, the remembered experience, good or bad, retains a place within the mind. But those experiences also retain a place within the body—body memory, so to speak. With that body memory, the cells release an energy, sometimes negative. It can impact the muscles, the stress centers, the vascular system, the elimination system, the immune system—every cell within the body. Why do you think you say, *he gives me a pain in the neck*, or *get off my back*, etc., etc? It is because you know that your body is affected. So if you understand this, then it is easier to immediately let go of that negative energy when you feel it charging up within the mind or body.

Now, that is where the benefits of therapy, meditation, massage, acupuncture, and other techniques for balancing the body can be great. If you find that you have negative energy at work in your body, then each of you find a comfortable way to eliminate it.

If the fear of intimacy is intensified by events of rejection, abuse, lack of love from the past of one partner, then the other partner can be a big help by a gentle application of love, kindness and understanding. Often it can help to discuss those past feelings. But in doing so, it has to be done with complete acceptance and trust on the part of both parties. How do you establish that trust? You do it with loving allowance, respectful communication, and responsibility. No judgment. And you do it privately, in a quiet, warm atmosphere.

One of the greatest reasons for the breakdown of a loving relationship is lack of respect. By using the three principles, you have no lack of respect. Not far behind, is thinking yourself a victim. When you can understand that you are never the victim, loving allowance for each of you to be, jumps into place.

If the two can look at and carefully study their illusion of separation, they will learn a lot about each other and *themselves*. If they recognize and admit their fears, they will each find the fears will begin to dissolve as they speak them. When that happens, they can again gaze into the eyes of their lover, with the eyes of a lover. Love becomes paramount in their relationship.

Linda: Thank you. A friend told me that you once told him that a relationship has to be one hundred percent for both, not fifty-fifty. I've always believed that a good relationship is two people standing side by side, heart to heart.

Dr. Peebles: Ah, yes, Linda. You are a wise woman. Yes, it will only work if each gives one hundred percent. It is not really a matter of giving, but of being there one hundred percent. In every way, to the fullest. It means making no demands, having no expectations—a sharing of love, a sharing of caring, a sharing of respect. It is only then that you have a loving relationship. Anything less is an illusion.

In that loving relationship, between lovers, whether it be male and female, or of the same sex, to achieve real intimacy, to reach the most beautiful and highest order of sexuality, there has to be complete surrender. And I mean complete. To reach that place of complete surrender, there has to be complete trust. Now, in a new love relationship that may take a little time to achieve but when it is reached, the wait will be worth every minute. The expression of true, deep love encompasses a completeness, a merging of souls, a universal dance of oneness.

Linda: (Laughing)…Don and I called it cosmic sex, cosmic love.

Dr. Peebles: Ah! Don is laughing, too. He agrees! Ah, yeah. See, in order to achieve that place, the fear of intimacy has to be released. The illusion of separation has to be recognized as only an illusion, and love and respect fill the soul. Yes.

Linda: It seems that various religious and social ideas have stifled our human sexuality. I suppose we've allowed it to do that but there seems to be much confusion about that in the public and private mind.

Dr. Peebles: Yes. One of the greatest needs of mankind is to be loved and to love. It tends to be the nature of religion to suppress passion because it is believed that passion leads to sin and criminal activity and the purpose of religion is to achieve purity in life, to do away with sin. So they believe that in order to achieve purity, one has to take away passion.

But it is the experience of the soul to desire passion, to reach out in such a way to bring love toward oneself, to express love for another. At a soul level, it is seen in all its purity, in all its beauty. The soul has a deep desire to achieve passion, for in so achieving, the soul finds oneness. And it is in that expression where the greatest inspiration, the greatest works of art, the greatest music, find their beginning. It is within that spark of the divine where the beauty of life evolves and unfolds for the world.

All great religious masters, such as Jesus, taught love. Is it not a paradox that the outflowing religious bodies have a fear of love and passion? They tend to enforce the illusion of separation, condemnation, judgment, isolation from others, and from God. They move toward greater separation rather than trying to dissolve the separation. A paradox that could stand some scrutiny, I would say.

The religious doctrine is in a constant battle with the human heart. In the future, human sexuality will be looked upon in a different light. The beauty of it will not be denied or feared and it will be looked upon with respect, reverence and thanksgiving. The greatest achievements of mankind have come from passion. Sexuality is a dance of God.

Linda: While speaking of sexuality, especially in today's world, one cannot help but think of AIDS. Will you speak of that?

Dr. Peebles: Ah, yes. That disease, or any other disease which is transferred by sexual activity, has nothing to do with sexuality itself. It has to do with judgment and fear of sexuality. The disease has manifested as a result of the fears, social mores and attitudes. It is only a reflection of social conditions in your world. It is a disease that is at war, just as your society tends to be at war. A mirror image. Yes, it has had an impact on the sexual life of your day, and will continue to do so for awhile, so self-responsibility is important. But more so, is the understanding that the disease is there to teach some important lessons to do with fear and with unconditional love. You either choose to continue to live in fear, or you reach out with compassion and unconditional love. I say to each of you, it will strike close to you and then you will have the opportunity to make your choice. Fear?—or unconditional love?

Do not think of it as a homosexual disease, for it is a disease for all of you. It has given you the opportunity to look at sexual diversity—and to come to a new understanding of that. Heterosexuals and homosexuals both have a little to learn. When I speak of sexuality, I speak of the internal attitudes, not the physical representation, and each of you embody both male and female. Ultimately, it is desirable to think of yourself as bisexual in nature but that in no way needs to be expressed in a physical way. You are all the same, all sexual beings, all spiritual beings, no matter the physical body you have chosen to present yourself in this time.

All of you need to look at others, no matter their sexual identity, as the very same. Learn to express love for one another, male or female, heterosexual or homosexual, without fear. Give another human being a hug and do not question their sexual identity, do not think of it as a sexual experience, think of it as one soul to another soul. You all have things to learn about each other.

In order for any relationship to be good, it first takes a good relationship with the self. When you are comfortable within, then you are comfortable without. The relationship will not be based on the fear that in order to be in the relationship you have to give up a part of yourself. Your needs will be met within the partnership because you have already met them. You do not sit around waiting for the other to fill some emptiness or need within yourself. The other does not complete you. You are complete, you see. And with that completeness, with being there one hundred percent, there is no threat, no expectation, no need for control, only a complimentary union which enhances.

But remember, you are here to experience, and you learn from each relationship, from each expression of sexuality, from each bond of love, no matter if you are able to reach genuine intimacy or tear away the illusions of separation. Just in reaching out, allowing yourself to touch and be touched, you have gained. You have stroked your canvas of life, you have held the paintbrush in your hand, and you have been the creator.

Linda: Thank you, Dr. Peebles.

Dr. Peebles: Thank you and God bless each and every one of you as you dance God's dance of intimacy and sexuality. Make romance a daily occurrence, embrace your sexuality, surrender to all the nuances as you create the beauty which is so abundant. And remember, appreciation for the beauty and magic of life begins within your mind. Enjoy the challenges which you create, learn from them, allow happiness to be yours. It is always your choice. Always.

My friends, go your ways in peace, love and harmony. Life is a joy. Never are you the victim, always the eternal creator. Create your reality by letting go of fear. Dance the dance of intimacy not only with others, but with your *self*. That is where you will find fulfillment and joy beyond your wildest dreams and imagination. That is where you will be one with God, one with all. God bless you each and every one.

11

PERSPECTIVE FROM THIS SIDE OF THE VEIL

o o o o o o o o o o o o o o o o o o o o o o o o o o o o o o o
"Life is a creative adventure!"

—The grand spirit, Dr. Peebles

In January of 1996, in the midst of my grief following Don's death three months earlier, I received a letter from Dr. Fred Bader, Ph.D., in which he wrote, "I just finished your book, *To Dance With Angels.* I was absolutely blown away."

He noted that he would like to talk with us. I telephoned Dr. Bader at his Fairfield, Connecticut, office. I informed him of Don's recent death and discovered that Dr. Bader was a thanatologist and specialized in grief therapy. We spent quite awhile discussing grief issues, our mutual belief in eternal life, in addition to the psychology of Dr. Peebles which Don and I had presented in our book. Dr. Bader had an interest in a personal session with Dr. Peebles so I referred him to medium, Athena Demetrios.

Fred Bader checked in on me a couple of times over the months to see how I was doing on my journey through grief. His personal concern and professional insight was most helpful to me.

Knowing that Dr. Bader not only incorporates the spiritual psychology of Dr. Peebles into his personal life but also into his professional life, I felt it would be of value to my readers to ask him to contribute to my book.

Dr. Bader has worked for more than twenty-five years as a psycho-therapist. He currently has a general practice of psychology in Fairfield, Connecticut, sixty miles outside New York City. His credentials are most impressive. He holds a Ph.D. in Clinical Psychology, a Master's and Bachelor's Degree in Psychology. As a thanatologist, he works therapeutically and educationally with the terminally ill, their families and their grieving survivors. He is also a Board-certified Sex Therapist and Relationship Counselor. His professional affiliations include Supervisor and Fellow, American Academy of Clinical Sexologists; Clinical Fellow, American Academy of Clinical Sexologists; Clinical Supervisor, American Academy of Clinical Sexologist; American Board of Sexology; Certified Marriage Counselor; Clinical Member, American Association of Marriage and Family Therapists; Clinical Member, American Association of Sex Educators, Counselors and Therapists; Clinical Member, American Psychology Association; and Clinical Member, Connecticut Psychology Association.

As a leading authority in the area of relationship enhancement, sexuality, intimacy and love, Dr. Bader has appeared as a guest on television and radio shows dealing with topics having to do with intimacy issues and has been a columnist and contributing writer for various publications. He has hosted his own radio show and he has a national-international telephone counseling service. He has structured *"More Love"* relationship workshops and holds workshops on death and the after-life.

Dr. Bader is co-author of *A Life Remembered*, a book used primarily in funeral homes as a give-away to mourners. Family and friends of the deceased, who come during the wake or funeral can record personal memories of the deceased so the family can have a lasting record of their loved one's life.

He is Founder and Director of *The Love Foundation, Inc.*, a non-profit organization whose mission is to help create and contribute to a more loving society by various acts of kindness and care.

Also a member of an international group of researchers, INIT—the International Network for Instrumental Transcommunication—he is an active member of the United States branch of that organization. INIT deals with electronic communication from the other side.

In regards to his work as a thanatologist, Dr. Bader states, "My mission on the death and dying side is to dispel the myth of death, and eliminate, or certainly alleviate, the *fear* of death. I'd like to go public, like many of us, to move somewhat out of the esoteric circles and the New Agers and move more and more toward middle America to help people understand what is really happening with regards to our lives, why we are here, and what happens once we leave the body, time and time again. Currently, I have a work in progress which will deal more extensively with the whole process of dying and what lies ahead in regards to multi-dimensionality and life eternal.

"I plan to integrate my '*More Love*' workshop experiences together with my understanding of death and dying for those who have lost people. I want to help people move more efficiently through their own grieving process by relating to those who have left the body, to better understand what the process is, and, of course, that life is eternal."

Here we find two exceptional doctors, Fred Bader and James Martin Peebles, one on this side of the veil and one on the other side, both reaching out with love to share their ideas, philosophy and wisdom in an attempt to heal those in need. Dr. Bader was kind enough to give me his thoughts regarding the value of Dr. Peebles' spiritual psychology and how effective it can be when put to use.

In Dr. Bader's words: "I'd like to begin with the illusion of separation. In the beginning sessions I had with Dr. Peebles over the last couple of years, every time there had been a reference to the illusion of separation my own understanding of that concept was as a separation from our fellow man and from other life forms, and that fairly much was my understanding for a period of time. But then more recently, I began to really understand the full meaning of the concept.

"The separation illusion is really about being separated from God. What really brought my attention to this was the *I AM* doctrine in which I have some experience and am pretty well versed. Fundamentally, the God-within is a related concept here. We are really never separated from God, God is in all life. The truly amazing thing, and the more expansive viewpoint, is that God is everywhere.

"In all the myriad of ways that Dr. P. references the illusion of separation, within all the different contexts that he presents this concept in his readings, it is always so pertinent and strikes such a deep chord in me because *knowing*—I think this is the key here—*knowing* that we have God inside of us, gives great power to our understanding but even more so to the whole notion that we create our own reality at all times. Even in the density and lowered vibration of these earthly bodies, we have the great potential to create, and we do create whatever it is that we want, good and bad and everything in-between. So thinking that we are never separated from God, the God-within, we have so much more control over our living experience.

"The separation illusion, of course, is running rampant within society. So often, the more mainstream religions teach that God is separate from us, and is some entity somewhere in some other dimension. But I think I should say I *know* that is one of the grandest illusions of all. We are *never* separated. God is in us and affects all that we do.

"On a practical note, in my clinical practice, a handful of patients that I work with have really come into their own. Their original reasons for working with me has been altered to some degree and, in some cases, to a sufficient degree, in a direction toward greater spiritual understanding and manifestation on a personal level. Several of them have been very, very tuned into the I AM and it really has changed their lives profoundly.

"When we arrive at the understanding that we live forever, that you can't kill us, which happens to be one of my favorite statements, we *remember* what we all *know* as souls and we gain a fuller awareness. It is so wonderful to watch the people I work with emerge from a certain level of understanding into a tremendously expanded opportunity and ability to see themselves as part of a much larger universe. They also have control once they recognize that God is within. It is amazing the kind of empowerment it creates for people.

"This inspirational concept is one of the most powerful concepts for all of us to understand, to know just how connected we are and that separation, in fact, is an illusion, that all life is connected to all life and whatever happens to one aspect of life happens to all of life everywhere. It's a great improvement on the old notion that comes around here and there with different social climates, in terms of social activism and understanding.

"People coming together certainly was a tenant or a concept that was brought forward during the social revolution in the late sixties, early seventies. But I think coming around into the nineties now through the turn here, more and more people are waking up to multi-dimensionality and so important in that is the separation illusion issue.

"So once again, from my perspective, Dr. Peebles, loving James Peebles, heard the information and passed it on, and I, in my own way, as you, Linda, and others, will pass the information along to others.

"Now, regarding Dr. P.'s three principles. I have to say that all three principles are tremendously powerful and the concept of using them in tandem is certainly wonderful and so appropriate. Let's take them in order. *Loving allowance for all things to be in their own time and place starting with yourself.* Well, this is the very premise for my work in therapy. Basically, we talk about self-love and, of course, other love. This concept is about tolerance, tolerating other people and the differences. I do a good amount of relationship work with marriages and other forms and configurations of relationships, but so often people operate under the myth that we should be the same, the partners should be the same, have the same interests. They come in often times with the expectation that Dr. Bader is going to help them become the *same* and that always makes me chuckle. What I tell them right off the bat, usually in the first session as I'm structuring my work with them, is, 'you know, the concept here is not to be the same but is to really acknowledge the differences and to appreciate and honor the differences.'

"That's what makes for successful relationships, and I'm sure you'll agree, Linda. Dr. Peebles and his infinite wisdom. I love this man as I know you do. I'm so tickled by the opportunity to help and be part of your process and your project and privileged to be part of him and his work.

"This concept of loving allowance for all things to be in their own time and place starting with yourself—respecting development, respecting the differences and respecting yourself, is an important part of all my work. The application of the last piece here, starting with *yourself*, obviously is to love yourself enough to appreciate your own developmental process and where you are along the time-line, the experience line—and to respect the fact that you're engaged in process. This important concept is two prong, appreciating yourself and your own development, but also appreciating others. The whole notion of judgement—helping one to be less judgmental, respecting each individual process and having that projected out to the world, respecting others and their process in their own time and place is such an important principle. It is even more profound when you understand multidimensionality.

"Certain people, of course, have a better understanding than others. In my own work with those handful of folks that I was referencing before—those people who understand that life is eternal, that life goes on and on and on—they understand that this is a task that we all must learn. It is a developmental task for the soul and, like most things, putting it off just means that there is more work to be done, which is fine, too, but it is understanding and respecting that there *is* more work to be done. So the beauty here of this profound concept is that we respect *our* process, we respect *the* process.

"In a more expanded view, if you look again at multi-dimensionality and life eternal, then we will need to respect our lives and our process of learning over and over and over again, throughout time. That's

really what it is, respecting people's developmental pathway and allowing them to learn what they need to learn. And in a more spiritual way,
to support and respect them in their process of why they are here time
and time again, lifetime after lifetime, and to allow them their lessons.

"*Increased communication with respect for life, starting with yourself.*
Wonderful principle. I do so much couple work, so much work with
relationships, and so much of what I do is teaching people how to
communicate. In looking at those two first words, *increased communication*, I'm thinking, my God, this is exactly where I place so much
emphasizes in my professional life, and incidentally, in my personal life
as well. I do try to 'walk the walk' or 'walk the talk,' however it's
expressed. I do try to live what I expound and I am a good communi-
cator and do apply what I teach others to my own life, more so now
than ever. I can't say that this was always the case, I must honestly con-
fess.

"So what is the applicability to this principle? There are a number of
ways of interrupting increased communication but for me I interrupt it
at the most concrete level. Increased communication works two ways,
information coming in and information going out. I think that in my
work it is so important to help people communicate what it is they
need from each other and to communicate as openly as possible. The
reference here, starting with yourself, is back to the *I* first, to be able to
integrate within oneself the desire and also the respect, if you will, to
open one's self up to life. And to me it really is opening to life.

"With communication skills comes the understanding that one has
the right to take the information in. Let me speak for a moment about
at least one aspect of that. That would be the whole notion of penetra-
tion. I'm sure you're aware of that terminology with Dr. P. Though it
sounds as if it's a direct sexual reference to sexuality, it certainly is
much broader than that. The ability to be able to receive and to give, to
take information in, has a lot to do with realizing that you're entitled
to communicate, to give the information out and to express the information, but, also, to be able to receive the information, to be pene-

trated by the information, to be open to others and their point of view. It's that exchange, a dance, a communication dance, if you will. So to me it's tremendously important in my work and will continue to be with the newer work which I'm developing. Very important.

"Let's move on to number three. *Self-responsibility for your life as a creative adventure. For never in your life are you the victim, always the creator.* I can't help but do the last piece because I've heard it so often from him and it's so inspiring and it touches me so deeply.

"I don't want to rate these principles but I have to tell you that probably this third principle is the one I have used most in my work with people in the last year or two. My work always spills over into my personal life and I've used these principles with my wife. Especially number two...and I've learned the lessons of number one in recent years. So there is a personal reference and application for me as well.

"*Self responsibility for one's life as a creative adventure.* That is so amazing—victimhood and then creation—the basic concept or tenant that we create our own reality all the time, that we are never the victim.

"In my work as a psychologist so often people feel victimized. They come to me feeling very victimized, very angry, all the corresponding feelings—sadness, feeling unempowered, a sense of worthlessness, on and on and on. So often they're feeling like a victim. What most people do not understand is that we create it all, although I think they're waking up to this and you're going to help them with this new book, Linda, but of course you know that.

"When we come into body we come in with our circumstances basically laid out, with our mission in check or in hand, so to speak, ready to go, to create our own reality. And even with that, given the concept of free will, we're always free to change and move in any way that we want. So we're always the creator, never, ever, ever the victim.

"That understanding has been so important for me at both a personal level and certainly in my professional life. I have taught this to so many, many people. Let's look at the first piece of this. If we are creators of our own experiences and not the victims of those experiences then whatever happens that may be uncomfortable is something we've created. Why would we create it? Of course, we create it for the learning opportunity, the proverbial dusting ourselves off, picking ourselves up. Pain is a grand teacher and we know, a divine intervener or coming in to help us learn and grow in ways that otherwise maybe we wouldn't. So, to see ourselves as victim doesn't give us a full opportunity for learning. And in many cases, it ignores the learning opportunity. Seeing ourselves as creators, even with the pain associated at times with what we create and what we experience, seeing ourselves as having the ability to learn from those experiences, is a wonderful, wonderful thing. I teach that a lot in my work.

"A direct application of that is helping people see the great value in what they create, and taking responsibility. It is always an opportunity for growth when they see themselves as creator and not victim. It also empowers them and so often allows them to continue on their pathway and to be less concerned with making mistakes. It gives them strength, and, in a certain way, freedom knowing that they are no longer victim. It allows them to move forward in a more efficient way, perhaps in a more expeditious way, because they seem to be less afraid, at least in my experience. It allows people to move forward, to be more willing to create and even enjoy the whole process of creation. Being the victim is passive and being the creator is more active. *Self-responsibility for your life as a creative adventure.* I see this over and over again in my work. So many people don't want to take responsibility and would rather feel victimized by life. Once they understand that responsibility is theirs for what they created—ah, the creation side—they can then see themselves not as victims anymore but now as creators. Creator of what?—the last piece, creator of the adventure of their lives. They are able to create really whatever it is that they want. Free will acting as it does, they are able to move forward whether it is somewhat generated, if not significantly so, by one's life's mission. But they do have freedom of choice, and they go forward unafraid, knowing that it's okay to fall, it's okay to skin their knees as Dr. P. may say, or has referenced before, certainly to me more than a few times. They can pick themselves up, dust themselves off and continue to move forward in their development and growth.

"There lies great beauty—the permission and freedom to move forward. In my work with patients, helping them with this concept, I think I act in a certain way to help them give themselves permission, if you will, for forward movement, to move forward with less fear, with more hope, and to look forward to a large degree to new adventures which they create for themselves. So, this third concept is tremendously important as are the first two.

"I would say in a quick summary about all three principles that these principles have become more integrated into me, in my understanding, and they've become more and more manifested in all areas of my own life and tremendously useful to those I work with. I continue to build the foundation of each principle and the seminars I am developing very much integrate these principles. I'll be talking about Dr. P.'s principles and the manifestation of these principles as a big part of my work.

"After all, Linda, it is all about love, isn't it? That's the simple, profound piece. It's all about love and that's really how I'm going to try and do my part, teaching that."

Yes, Fred, it *is* all about love. Simply and profoundly. Love is a four letter word which each of us need to speak more often. In fact, it might not be a bad idea to shout it out to the world from every mountaintop!

And, from the pen of James Martin Peebles, many, many years ago: "Love is the deepest and mightiest principle in the universe—the silvery sea over which mortals sail to the heaven they seek."

12

DUMPING THE GARBAGE

○ ○
"Guilt drives people to be deaf, dumb and blind to their own drives, hopes and fears and wants, bias and prejudices therein."

—*The grand spirit, Dr. Peebles*

Guilt feelings come from many sources and can be a very complicated emotion. One form of guilt can be best described as the result of holding onto anger so long that it turns inward. And what is anger? Hurt.

A person who suffers guilt may feel unworthy, remorseful, cruel, self-hating and negative. Not only do they wallow in their own negativity but it will usually affect all who come in contact with them. Often because the person who carries guilt cannot identify his real feelings, he may lash out inappropriately and make life miserable for everyone including himself.

When one can understand that we all have a desire to be loved, when we become aware of the *illusion* of separation and the fear of intimacy that comes with our earthly territory, we can then put into practice the three principles and feelings of hurt, anger, guilt and the resulting depressions should immediately fade from our lives.

Many people carry with them all the emotional baggage that has piled up over the years. They hold onto their abuse, real or imagined, and allow it to burden their mind, their emotions, sometimes to the point of holding them prisoner. They become stuck in the past emotion, refusing to let it go, refusing to move forward, refusing to forgive others or even themselves. Life becomes joyless, empty, and even angry.

And as Dr. Peebles stated in the opening chapter quote, they become blind to life. One can become so swallowed up by victimhood that other choices are not even evident or even dreamed possible. But as Dr. Bader told us, when one moves out of victimhood and regains his or her power it is transformational.

Dr. Peebles will now share with us his wisdom of how we may regain our power when it somehow has been lost.

Linda: Hello, Dr. Peebles. I received your message that you wanted a chapter on guilt. I would also like to talk about the emotional baggage that many carry with them throughout their lives.

Dr. Peebles: Ah, Linda, God Bless you. It is as always a joy to share some insight with you and, of course, with those of you who will be reading my words. God Bless you all. We will discuss letting go, *dumping the garbage*, so to speak, the garbage that many of you carry around with you. Yeah. It would be a much lighter load when you come over here if you could let all of it go while still in the body.

The inability to let go is of course enshrouded in the illusion of separation. We have talked earlier about forgiveness and I believe that we emphasized that forgiveness really begins with one's self. The result of not forgiving oneself is pain, resentment, anger, guilt. But those are lessons, and only by embracing the pain, expressing the anger in some non-violent way, and by respectful communication, often only with self, can those emotions be released. *Oh, but Dr. Peebles I don't want to embrace the pain.* I say to you that you must embrace it, if only for a moment. The pain will say to you, '*Oh, see, I am not so bad. I bring to you new understanding.*' By embracing the pain you then take responsibility that you have created it, you have stroked your canvas of life with your own paint brush. You also then allow *yourself* love—to *be* in your own time and place—and that is forgiveness of self. When you have reached that place of forgiving yourself, you can then reach out to others with forgiveness, new communication, new understanding. You open to life, encourage an echo, allow diversity of thought and action and, yes, even enjoy it. You dance the dance of life, and you're lighter. The garbage has been tossed aside and it no longer weights you down and unduly encumbers your life.

Guilt is often used as a manipulative tool by those who feel the need to control others. Do you allow them that control by taking on guilt feelings as they feed them to you? Do you allow them to have power over you? If someone says to you that you are worthless do you indeed become worthless and do you doubt who you are? If the illusion of separation tends to be a reality in your life, then you will feel less than you are. If you do not love yourself, then you will believe that no one can love you, that you do not deserve to be loved. You will become the passenger of your life, not the pilot. You will feel the victim, victimized.

Ah, yes, it sometimes feels good to be the victim—as victim, one does not have to take any responsibility for feelings and actions, right? But if you allow guilt and victimhood to have control of your life you will not be free, you will not love yourself, and then how can you give love to others. Do you understand?

Linda: Very much so. I found something you wrote many, many years ago in your earthly life and I want to use it here, if you don't mind?

Dr. Peebles: Yes, go ahead. My pen was very prolific in those days.

Linda: Yes, it was. I do have to say that you seemed as wise then as now, from your place in the world of spirit.

Dr. Peebles: Thank you, my dear. I was lucky enough to recognize many truths in my earthly life. I did have my band of angels guiding me and I might say, often encouraging me to examine my attitudes carefully. I could be a stubborn one, yeah. *Obstinate* might be a better choice of words there, yes. But often, with encouragement, I would see a different light on the subject, gain a new understanding. I, too, just as each of you, had many lessons to learn—and I too, had many lifetimes to learn those lessons. And who knows, maybe one day I might jump back into the body and see what challenges await me. For now, I am having too much fun and joy communicating with all the beautiful souls on earth who come across my teachings and guidance. I delight in sharing with each of you. It is a dance of love, a dance of joy. Remember, I learn from all of you, as I hope you learn from me. That is the core issue. We teach one another. So, Dr. Peebles is not perfect by any means. It is a sojourn of love and enlightenment which we all embark upon, indeed. But thank you for your kind words, Linda.

Linda: You're welcome. This is what you wrote more than a hundred years ago.

Dr. Peebles: One hundred years—a wink of the eye.

Linda: "The oak remembers not each leaf it bore; and yet each leaf and bough and brawny limb help to make up the towering tree. Many of the acts and minor events of our lives have died out, or cease to echo in the memory chambers of our souls; still, their results live in our characters. Let then, be forgotten! It is not wise to brood over the broken rounds of the ladder our feet just pressed. The summit of the temple is to be reached. Direct the eye upward, and press forward towards the higher altitudes of heavenly truth and wisdom.

"The toiling seamstress remembers not each stitch she took in the garment; and yet, every stitch helped to make up that garment; and so each thought, word, purpose, and deed, help to make up the real life of the soul; and backward-looking memory, tracing the effects, may—ay, must construct a mirror before which we shall be necessitated to stand, face to face with ourselves...We weave the moral garments in this life that shall in quality clothe us when entering the future state of existence."

Dr. Peebles: Hmm, much wisdom there, indeed. I did not refer to events as lessons as I now do but I would suppose my meaning is exact.

Life is an upward movement toward heavenly truths, a remembering so to speak of our spiritual nature, a fulfilling of our soul, and it is true that every thought, every movement, every action and deed, become part of our very soul, at least in a deductive sense. It is the reflection in the mirror which enables one to have new understanding of self. I still agree with all that I wrote as one has to let go of the backward-looking memories in order to continue on a smooth path toward enlightenment. There is no point in retracing or brooding over where one has walked. The movement is forward and upward. To stop on one broken round of the ladder and to not step beyond to the next, stifles. Do you understand?

Linda: Perfectly. I also opened this chapter with one of your more recent heavenly quotes which I think you are familiar with.

Dr. Peebles: Ah, yes. When one becomes blinded to life, closed to the echoes, the beauty of life becomes absent, silent, and fear takes hold. Fear of diversity, fear of love and intimacy, and the illusion of separation becomes overwhelming. Guilt disables, lowers self esteem, reduces hopes, kills dreams, destroys creativity, alters the ego to the point that self worth suffers tremendously. So what do you do about it? You release it by realizing that you don't need it any longer. It becomes a lesson learned. When you accept that you created that place, you also realize that you can create another place, one free of guilt, full of joy, full of love.

When one is faced with looking at all that garbage, what many refer to as baggage, recognize that it no longer serves you. And in all probability, the person who may have been the *reason* for your baggage, that is, in your *own* mind, has probably not even given you any thought, or the event any thought, so why do you continue to carry it with you? Remember, your world is your very own perception. You have the choice to perceive it as you wish. And if you wish to be the victim, so be it. But if you wish to be the pilot of your life, the one at the wheel, so to speak, then consider that you can shift your perception, let go, forgive, and move forward.

Linda: At times, when I have become aware that someone is so wrapped up in guilt it has been somewhat of a struggle to help them reach that understanding that guilt does nothing for them, and in many ways only invalidates their life experience. They *are* blind to life, because they are so caught up in the past that there is no way they can enjoy and really experience the present. We do all suffer some kinds of what we would consider abuses throughout our lives, and we can find it easy to hang onto anger and resentments.

Dr. Peebles: Yes. Many do hang on to past events and find a comfort zone by doing so. But it is not a comfort zone of peace, it is a zone of emotional turmoil, powerlessness, lack of joy, and most probably, lack of love. For some, they find it to be a place of manipulation, as I mentioned. It is also a place of denial. They look at their world as one of separateness, out of control, albeit an illusion. Their world is not out of control, they just refuse to take creative control, creative responsibility. If it can be brought to their attention that they have the power within themselves to take hold of their lives, that the past is just that, they then can return to the present with much enthusiasm and look forward to the adventures that the future holds. By holding onto the pain of the past no one, except themselves, suffer. And that suffering can take on many forms, be it physical, mental or emotional. If one understands that you ventured into the school earth for lessons, that you chose your families, many of the events of your life, all as lessons to be learned, you can then accept all things that happen in your life as delightful opportunities for growth. At the time, they may not seem as opportunities, but in the larger soul picture, they are, indeed. Delightful opportunities, yes.

Linda: So you are saying that by hanging onto this baggage, refusing to let it go, it is one way of not accepting that the particular lesson is over—time to move on to another?

Dr. Peebles: Yes, you could say that. By understanding that the experience is nothing but a lesson in growth, one can let it go, move on to another, and another wonderful opportunity for growth. And life is full of them. Each lesson gives us new found inspiration, understanding, and breaks down the illusion of separation. You will discover not only that you are never alone, but that God is supporting your every movement, albeit in your eyes as not the best of movements. You are each doing the best you can at any given moment. The lessons of life are complicated, the fears you have brought into this life are a challenge to overcome. Life is all about learning about your soul, learning about relationships, letting go of your fear of intimacy, embracing the spiritual essence of every soul. A challenge, yes. But also a joy as you move closer to the God essence in your journey to the heart of your soul. Unconditional love, not only for yourself, but for God, for every man, woman, and child who walks the earth, and for all who live in other dimensions is the mission of life. It is also the foundation of the universe. Love for each and every one of God's creations. That is the movement of the universe—the spiral of love, which enfolds, embraces, All that Is.

Linda: I have a question about self-love. When you say that to someone their immediate reaction may be that self-love feels like a selfish act—a self-centeredness. I personally do not see it that way but would say something about that to give those who do feel that way an understanding. I think guilt feelings come into play there. If you think of yourself first, you may feel guilty.

Dr. Peebles: Yes, you are right. Many do look at self-love *first*, as a selfish act and in turn feel guilty if they do put themselves first. I believe we have discussed this to some degree. It is not a selfish act. In order to love another, one has to love oneself. Clearly, openly, and unconditionally. Again, a challenge. And yes, guilt feelings can take hold as you say to yourself, *I shouldn't be thinking of myself first—my desires, my hopes, my fears.* But only by recognizing those things first within yourself can you respect and allow them in another. A paradox?—*if I take care of my desires, what does that do to that other person?* What it does is to give honesty to the relationship, disallows guilt feelings and resentments, does not have any expectations, allows for respectful communication, and permits love to be exchanged.

Linda: Guilt often seems to come about from fears of not having someone's approval or love, such as a parent, does it not?

Dr. Peebles: Very much so. The child seeks approval, love. When it is denied and not offered openly, the child may decide that it is his own actions that are responsible. He may decide that he is not good enough, can never live up to the expectations of the parent, so may come to the conclusion that he is not deserving. Those emotions may continue to hang on through childhood and into adulthood. Often, that can lead an adolescent or young adult toward a promiscuous search for love and approval, albeit a hollow victory. For others, they create a relationship with a spouse or lover that intensifies their own belief that they are not deserving of love, or that everything "wrong" with the relationship is their fault, not the other's. There we often have the abusive relationship which only tends to intensify the lack of self esteem, feelings of self doubt and worthlessness. They become convinced that no matter what they do, no one will approve. That can become the basis for the cycle of abuse. The guilty person will promise to be better, the physical abuser will ask for forgiveness, carrying his own guilt for his inappropriate action, fears of both parties quietly intensify, only to explode again in the future, piling on more guilt. Both victims, both unhappy, fearing the echo, building greater illusions of separation, losing respect for themselves, and not having respect for the other. A cycle, yes. But a cycle that can be broken. And it can be broken by coming to terms with the lack of loving allowance present, beginning with self. Yes, self. So what you seek, love and approval, is within the self. One does not have to look outward, look within. There, you will find it.

Linda: Will you talk of the guilt that is generated by some religious dogma?

Dr. Peebles: A big one, yeah. Organized religion in many cases has afflicted many with guilt. One has to wonder why they take that action in presenting their religious understanding. For centuries the churches have used what one can call tactics of control. In their mistaken belief that in order to keep their churches filled and overflowing, they have to have power and control over their members—and they have found an easy way to do that by showering guilt over their members. They fail to see the real essence of spiritual belief. Control and power are unnecessary. The teachings of Jesus of Nazareth are about love—pure and simple. One does not have to have guilt to accept and honor those teachings.

Organized religion has its constraints. True religious belief, spiritualism, which so many are searching for, can be found in the heart of the soul and the connection with the Christ-energy, which radiates nothing but love. Yeah, pure and simple.

But for some, they find comfort in the religious dogma that does have constraints and control, because they might find it easier to be guided by others, they may feel unworthy of grace, and have not come to a full understanding that God's love is there for all, no matter their faults and shortcomings, (or if you want to refer to it as sins). It matters not to God. Each of you is perfect in His eyes. That is true unconditional love.

There is nothing to fear about God. No guilt or fear is necessary to an understanding of God. As you learn more about yourself and the aspects of your own spiritual nature, the more you learn about God. Each of you is a spiritual being and each of you is of God.

So lighten up and enjoy who you are. Let go of useless thoughts and emotions. Feel the pain, if only for a moment, and continue on your journey to the heart of your soul. That is your purpose for being on the Earth-school. As you complete each lesson, put it behind you. The important wisdom that was gained will become, and remain, a part of your eternal fabric. Open your eyes, listen to the melody of life, create a joyous dance and go your way in peace, love and harmony.

◆　　◆　　◆

Don and I met Anne Boss in the summer of 1992 in Sacramento, California, while on our way to Washington State for the wedding I mentioned earlier. She was introduced to us by our friend, Jay Halford. Although our initial meeting was brief, we both liked Anne immediately.

Anne was then on the brink of new spiritual discovery. A recently divorced mother of two grown children, and today a grandmother, Anne was to discover what many of us do, that the forties can be a time of exciting adventure. Anne and I have become close friends and I have enjoyed watching her enthusiasm for embracing new thoughts and ideas. She admits she was reluctant to embark on her new journey. She has offered to share some of her journey with us. In her own words:

"*To Dance With Angels* was introduced to me in 1992, by a very special person in my life, Joe (Jay) Halford. At that time the only thing I knew about channeling is that I certainly didn't believe in it. Joe had asked if I would read the book. I wanted to please him. I tried on five separate occasions but found I couldn't stay focused or retain any of it, so I finally gave up.

"About eighteen months later I walked over to the bookcase looking for something to read and found myself drawn to *To Dance With Angels*. It was time! This wonderful book began my journey into self discovery, the New Age, and my way to a new and special relationship with God.

"Joe and I had taken a trip to Los Angeles so Joe could do some writing with his friend, Michael. While enjoying the peace and sunshine in Michael's backyard, I finished reading the book and had quite an experience.

"Let me say here, I'm not a person that is able to take naps during the day and certainly not outside in the backyard of someone I hardly knew. I finished the last page and had such a wonderful sense of peace fill my whole body. Enjoying the moment, I leaned my head back on the lawn chair and closed my eyes. I instantly fell into a very deep sleep. When I awoke, it was like something had shifted and I felt contentment and very centered. It was like the wisdom of those words in the book had become a part of my whole being and I believe now, that's exactly what happened.

"A short time later, I became interested in meditation. I had been meditating for about two months when, during one particular meditation, Dr. Peebles' face appeared right in front of me. I was so surprised that I physically jumped back. I knew instantly it was Dr. Peebles, even though I had never seen a picture of him. I knew by his appearing to me that he was there to help me and he has been with me ever since.

"Loving allowance, beginning with myself, has rid me of a lifetime of guilt. I was raised thinking guilt was a badge of honor. I believed feeling guilty meant that I was a good person.

"What I have learned is how this way of thinking kept me from loving and respecting myself. But my guilt feelings also affected others. It kept my son from sharing with me his lifelong depression which led him to a suicide attempt in his early twenties. It prevented my daughter from sharing with me the fact that she had been date raped at an early age. Even though my kids and I have always been extremely close, more like best friends, they both had felt if they had shared this with me I would have felt guilty, somehow responsible. Later, they both were able to share this with me but only after they saw the change and growth in me and felt assured that I wouldn't feel guilty. Being able to share is what love is all about.

"Learning self-responsibility has actually been fun for me. It is very liberating. I feel I have always been a very responsible person and I was, but it keeps expanding as I grow. I used to believe being self responsible meant you owned up to any action you took or any words you spoke. I am constantly learning that it also has to do with who and where you are in life. It is always your choice as to how you react in any given situation. Relationships become more honest. My kids are more responsible for their own lives because Mom isn't fixing everything for them and the three of us appreciate the new honesty and openness of our relationships. Friend relationships are also changing because I say yes only when I want to and not because I need to be liked, or fear that I might disappoint someone. I used to say yes all the time and sometimes later would feel resentful. That isn't fair to either party.

"Increased communication has been very challenging for me in regards to my love relationship. This is a real challenge for me because of my fears—such as the fear of losing that person, not having his approval—and goes back to my early guilt issues. I'm still working on that aspect of myself.

"Communication with others has greatly improved. I see that increased communication seems to result from working the other two principles. I do know that applying all three principles results in more honest and open relationships."

◆   ◆   ◆

Now one would agree with Anne more than her beautiful twenty-eight year old daughter, Rhonda Boss. She relates for us what the recent changes she has seen in her mother has meant to her.

"The change in my mother has been incredible since she has lost the guilt and other baggage that the three principles has helped her to overcome.

"Our relationship had always been honest and open—or so we thought. We talked about things incessantly, always including each other in our lives. When Mom went through her 'spiritual' change, at first, I resisted. I didn't understand this new strength and sometimes abrupt honesty. After the initial transitional period I learned that I could be much more open and honest with her. Even though we thought we had a very open relationship, I hadn't realized how much I had actually kept from her about my life. I was so afraid that Mom would feel guilty about something bad that happened to me that I couldn't turn to her to help me through it, or even just to talk it out. This part of our relationship which seemed so subtle before became enormous now that we have this honesty.

"Self responsibility was something my brother and I were taught from childhood, through words, and now Mom is teaching us by example. She is there to support us through everything but she doesn't try to fix it anymore. The self responsibility that I've learned from her has increased our communication, opening up the lines between us to encompass all parts of our lives—good and bad—allowing my Mom to truly become my best friend. Thanks, Dr. Peebles."

I can only say that many, many of us thank Dr. Peebles for bringing new understanding into our lives. Somehow, his teachings allow us to gain insight, to enrich our relationships by those new discovered insights. As he often reminds us, earth life is a study in relationships, but it is the relationship with self which influences our relationships with all others. If we can expand ourselves, let go of past hurts, emotions, and *dump the garbage*, as Dr. Peebles would say, we may discover that our relationships with others will be greatly enhanced and expanded, also. It can lighten our hearts, and in turn, lighten the hearts of those we love.

13

SPIRITUAL FOOD

Many people in today's complex and sometimes chaotic world are searching for spiritual sustenance to satisfy their hunger for a meaningful life. Often we look outside ourselves to seek that which could easily be ours by looking into our own soul. Within our souls, we have the answers. We know.

We also know that we are not alone but that memory has been clouded by cultural and environmental elements in addition to the illusion of separation that we struggle to break through.

The majority of people are said to believe in God, and to do so takes faith. How do we know that God even exists? I personally believe that within our very soul we do know that God exits. But science has not shown us God, at least not in the physical, material sense. Science, though, has shown us many manifestations of God—our very DNA, the building blocks of life; the cosmos; the miracle of conception; and the unveiling of many other life mysteries. This tends to make our faith stronger and lend credibility to the idea that human life and the universe are not chaotic, accidental events. At least it does for most of us. Some will always believe that death ends life, that there is no divine force in the universe, and they may hold to that belief unless some mystical event changes their perspective.

Polls have pronounced that the majority of Americans also believe in angels. Do angels exist? You bet they do—with or without wings, it seems not to matter. An occasional spiritual presence has been experienced by many, many people. Many of those experiences moves one beyond faith to a place of conviction that reality is shared with spiritual beings of another dimension.

I have discovered a lot of people are often hesitant to share their mystical experiences with anyone for fear of someone thinking them crazy. I personally have had people share with me, for the first time ever, their mystical experiences. I often have been open enough about my own mystical, paranormal experiences and beliefs that they have felt "safe ground" in relating their own experiences.

For those who have doubts about the existence of the world of spirit, and for those who remain somewhat skeptical, I can only say that is okay. Possibly at some point in their lives they may have their own experiences such as a near-death experience, a visitation by a deceased family member, or the appearance of an angel. At that time they will "remember" and know for themselves. It is not my desire to try to alter anyone's belief system. My desire is only to share and, in doing so, to give renewed understanding, hope, and healing.

In *Seers of the Ages*, James Martin Peebles wrote, "Faith, differing essentially from mere belief, is graded upward from the more external to the divine, corresponding relationally to the outer and inner consciousness. The latter is closely allied to intuition. It is a glimmering from the star of destiny. Faith is essential to successful communication with ministering spirits. The adjustment of the spirit batteries, under this law, is most delicate and beautiful. The spirit has to employ our magnetic sphere—enters into *rapport* with us sympathetically—and if we are any ways deceptive and tricky, gloomy and unbelieving, our very mental and moral condition defeats the object; for then a pure and truthful spirit, who *would* communicate, finds it very difficult to reach our sphere, it being so magnetically repellant. *Honest* doubt does not imply *un*-faith; in fact, it *is* faith in embryo. The candid inquirer always gets light; for such a sphere attracts the angel who comes to bless 'the poor in spirit.' Faith, then, is rooted in innocency. 'Thy *faith* hath made thee whole.' How beautiful it is under the effulgence of this spiritual light! When our purpose is sincere, Faith-angels come, administering 'good tidings of good' to those who 'seek immortality—eternal life!'"

He also had this to say about faith. "Beautiful, truly, is a calm, abiding faith—faith in the measureless possibilities of humanity—faith in the governing guidance of the spiritual heavens—faith in the unchangeability of the divine laws, and faith in the ceaseless, outflowing love of the Infinite."

Faith is inherent in the human soul. It is personal and unique and I also believe that reasonable skepticism is healthy.

Dr. Peebles put it beautifully when he wrote, "How sweet and perfect the little child's faith in the parent; and how firm should be ours in the innate goodness of every human being!" I would bet today he would replace *human* with the word spiritual and not limit faith to only the earth being.

◆   ◆   ◆

Obviously, most of us have come to understand the power of prayer. Not only can our prayers be healing for others, but, of course healing for ourselves. I came across something Dr. Peebles had written about prayer that I found interesting. He wrote, "Golden the age when men will *do*, rather than *say* their prayers." *Do* our prayers. How often do we pray to God to feed the poor but we ourselves make no effort to feed the hungry? How often do we pray for peace yet scowl at cultural diversity? I think you get the drift. Maybe we really need to strive to move into that "golden age" Dr. Peebles wrote of—beginning with what our prayers reflect.

Prayer and meditation are important because they not only put us in touch with the divine forces but they put us in touch with ourselves. Within those quiet and peaceful moments we open our connection with the spirit world, allowing ourselves to receive messages of love and divine inspiration in addition to conversing with God, our angels, our deceased loved ones, and our spirit guides. It becomes a beautiful opportunity for spiritual enrichment. When we receive guidance during prayer or meditation, it comes to our uncluttered and still mind with clearness.

◆   ◆   ◆

Dr. Peebles: Goodness gracious. You ask, Linda, if I am here? I have been peeking over your shoulder while you have been typing these words of this chapter. Spiritual food—good.

Linda: (Laughing) I know you were here, but as always I said my prayer asking God directly for communication with you, and to surround us with light, love, peace and harmony. I felt your presence and Don's, too. I know you guys are hanging out with me. You don't fool me too often—I think.

Dr. Peebles: Ah, you would be surprised! Don visits you several times a day and sometimes I don't think you know he's there. He peeks at you. He says, "I wonder how Linda, my darling, is doing?"—and in a flash he is gone and by your side. Yes.

Linda: That's nice. I like to know he's by my side—I love that he checks in on me.

Dr. Peebles: Spiritual food—we will speak of spiritual food for the soul. As you have written, prayer and meditation is just that. Meditation, in its many forms, not only relieves stress; puts you in touch with your higher self, so to speak; but it allows for intellectual communication at a cellular level. Within that slightly altered state, much like the daydream state, the life force energy flows much freer throughout the body, and with the free energy flow the chakras come into balance, alignment. It is a time of cleansing and healing of the body and of the spirit.

Those of us over here love it when those of you over there meditate. It gives us something to do—an opportunity to give guidance and inspiration. Each of you have several spirit guides who work closely with you. So, meditation is the opportune time for us to communicate, through visual or auditory efforts. In the slightly altered state of meditation, you hear our messages with somewhat more clarity. It saves us from having to give you a kick with our spiritual boot. Yeah.

Now, for those of you wanting direct communication with spirit—your guides or angels—I would suggest that you have a pen and paper in your lap as you begin your meditation. I would also suggest to unplug your telephone, play soft, gentle music in the background, light a candle, and have the fragrance and beauty of fresh flowers or a lush, green plant nearby. And begin with a prayer of love. Ask that you be given only that of the highest order and for the highest good. Quiet the mind, relax the body. Breathe deeply, and then relax the rhythm of your breath. Listen for the whispers of spirit. Imagine you hear what they say. If you see pictures or symbols, open your eyes slightly and draw them on your sketch pad. Write your feelings upon the pad. If you have a question, ask, and listen for the answer. You may at first think you are imagining all that you hear or see. Be patient. Believe that you hear the words. Soon, you will understand that it is not your own voice that you are hearing, nor your own thoughts.

Within the dream state, often you come to this side. You leave the body and dance the dance of the angels. It is a time of communion, an opportunity of nurturing and uplifting of the soul, a sharing of inspiration and wisdom. This is achieved most often without your conscious knowledge but it can also be purposefully achieved. Before you go to sleep, put into place your choice to come over here. You will, as always, be welcomed with loving arms.

If you have a problem, I would suggest that you place it in the hands of God. Ask for His guidance in prayer. His angelic helpers, His messengers, will go into action.

Now, one of the greatest spiritual foods is knowledge. It comes in all consistencies, textures, flavors, and you can simmer it as long as you want. You can have it for your supper, savor as a dessert, sip as a fine cup of English tea, chew it as a cow chews her cud, gulp it down as a glass of lemonade on a hot, humid summer afternoon. It is obtainable in many ways, through the written word, through the spoken word and through your many modern means of communication technology. And once you encounter it, it can be held in the recesses of the mind, to be called upon whenever needed or desired. It can take you on many adventures, to places all over the world, to the historical past, to the world of technology and science, to the world of metaphysics, to the world of the great philosophers, poets, and literary masters. Knowledge brings new awareness, new dreams, inspiration. It enlightens and satisfies the soul, but it also can leave a craving for more. It is truly food for thought.

14

ENDINGS AND NEW BEGINNINGS

○ ○
"The old dies that the new may sing of birth, maturity, victory."

—James Martin Peebles, 1869

One of the most difficult abuses for most of us to understand is the sexual abuse of a child. Yet, far too many do understand it from the point of view of one of those children. The road to healing for them can be a difficult and long one. Many survivors of sexual abuse live in guilt, shame, and denial, and often may be in their thirties or forties before they come to a place of healing.

I believe one of the most dramatic stories of healing as a result of meeting Dr. Peebles is the story of Athena Demetrios' childhood sexual abuse.

For the last ten years or so, Athena has worked with Dr. Peebles in a very intimate way. She is a professional medium for the grand spirit. But Dr. Peebles has also worked with her in a very intimate way, leading her to a place of healing in her personal life. And for her, his influence has given her a new beginning. She again, shares with us her journey to healing but we will begin with her earlier story from our book, *To Dance With Angels*, in which Don and I wrote, "...we cannot think of Athena without whispering the prayer, 'God bless the child.'"

In Athena's words more than ten years ago:

"I am the middle child, one of seven children born into a dysfunctional, alcoholic environment. Poverty was a way of life, and I do believe we all lived in a state of mild unspoken panic. When I was six, I was raped, strangled, bound, and threatened into silence by a butcher knife held against my throat by my mother's alcoholic boyfriend, who lived in the root cellar of our basement. I experienced this over a dozen times, and suffered total memory loss, with the exception of one singular incident which I thought was a simple case of molestation, although I couldn't remember anything past a certain point. The memory of it was like watching a television program turn to snow.

"As a child I felt a thousand years old, trapped in a little kid's body, and I knew that life was serious business. If I could have spit in the face of God, I would have. I don't know how I knew He even existed. I just knew He did and I hated Him. I was born a soul searcher. Trying to understand why, and who I am, is just part of my nature.

"I carried into adulthood deep feelings of despair, anxiety, and depression. I felt powerless, hopeless, extremely separated from life, and suicidal, and I didn't even know why I felt like this. I couldn't feel from my waist down. I couldn't sleep on my back because I felt like I could be stabbed if I did. I didn't know how to have fun and I didn't know why memories of childhood affected me like being caught in a fog."

It was a dream that Athena had of going down some stairs trying to rescue a little girl out of a basement that prompted her to speak with Dr. Peebles about her memory of molestation. That was the beginning for her of moving through the shame, denial and anger, to a place of acceptance, and ultimately, forgiveness.

After that first discussion with Dr. Peebles about her molestation, she began to move forward.

"I chose hypnotherapy as my tool for exploration and healing. I've learned to walk through fire, so to speak. I've tapped into depths of rage and anger I never knew existed inside of me. I've grieved and cried more than I ever have in my life. I've accepted the loss of what I never had as a child, and I've learned to honor the process of pain and the steps involved in healing.

"Prompted by a dream, I returned to the house in Oregon where the rapes took place. I physically went back into the root cellar, and there within the blackness I forgave him and rescued the lost child who had been trapped in that basement for thirty-three years. I took back my power and became my own parent. I love that little girl and she is inside of me now...alive, and she was worth all the pain and agony, every bit of it.

"Releasing myself from victimhood was not easy. It was hardest to forgive my mother. She died this year and I didn't feel a thing. Not because I've turned off, but because I had already grieved so deeply for what I never had. At her memorial I read, 'Mother, I no longer hold you responsible for my experience of sexual abuse. I chose this experience as a soul to grow from. I am not a victim.'

"The impact of this healing has been dramatic. I can feel from my waist down now. I can sleep on my back. I respect and love my strength and courage. It's good to be alive and to know what self-love is. The deep depression is gone and I know that I am a powerful creator. I'll forever be grateful to Dr. Peebles, Thomas Jacobson, and Dr. Daniel Slavin."

What Athena was to discover was that her healing was still in process, further unfolding just as the days, months and years unfold. This is what she now shares with us, eleven years following her mother's death.

"My first encounter with Dr. Peebles began in 1982 when I heard him through his medium Thomas Jacobson on *Open Mind*, KABC Talk Radio. His effect on my psyche was electrical and thrilled me through and through. I fell in love with his wisdom, insight and humor and *I simply wanted more.*

"As synchronicity would have it, the following day while working on a commercial (I am a make-up artist by trade), I experienced an instant rapport with the actor. The conversation flowed effortlessly around metaphysics and he made the following statement to me: 'I just had the most incredible reading by this character named Dr. Peebles.' I could hardly contain my excitement and immediately contacted Thomas Jacobson. I was curious about certain writings that seemed to flow through me with great ease after meditation. They seemed almost ethereal. Dr. Peebles said that it was a beginning of a channeling state and that with my permission he would like to come through me.

"Shortly after my initial contact with Dr. Peebles, I remember that I awoke one night from a sound sleep still caught between two worlds unable to move a muscle as if in a deep alpha state, but aware of the physical dimension at the same time. I saw a ball of white light speeding toward me. As it entered my solar plexus I felt as if I had just gone over a massive speed bump in a car and my stomach was full of butterflies. I sat up in bed and started talking like Dr. Peebles—a Scottish brogue touched with my own Greek ancestry. I thought I was nuts. I was scheduled to have a private session with Thomas the following day and Dr. Peebles' comments about that event were as follows: 'Oh yah, Athena, that was me...I came to you my darling to help instill within you a sense of joy about being alive.' That was the beginning of my love affair with James Martin Peebles and it continues to this day.

"*A sense of joy about being alive*; my greatest illusion of separation. The problem was, internally I felt numb, dead, and as if I was just putting in my time until I could get off the planet. It was at the prodding of Dr. Peebles that I regress to my childhood to re-experience and explore the sexual abuse and trauma that I had blocked out from my conscious memory. 'It's timely,' he had said, 'and your teachers and I agree that you're strong enough. You will re-experience techniques and beliefs that you created that have had an impact upon your entire life. It will be wonderful, wonderful. It will help you understand the healer that you are in this life.'

"*Wonderful?* I thought—*if it's so wonderful, you get your translucent butt down here, Dr. Peebles, and do it for me.* Another delightful opportunity for growth.

"What I found most bizarre was that the exact dream of walking down the stairs into the basement that I had recounted to Dr. Peebles was a dream that I had some ten years prior. At that time, scribbled across the paper as an afterthought I had written the following words; 'I am not strong enough to do this yet, but some day I will be.' That piece of paper, a key to my subconscious, surfaced one week before my first appointment with Dr. Daniel Slavin.

"Because my defenses were so strong, hypnosis was the tool my therapist, Dr. Slavin, used to unlock Pandora's Box—and unlock Pandora's Box we did.

"I did re-experience projecting out of the body, floating and observing the rapes, wanting to die and to go back in spirit. I re-experienced the exact moment when I created a wall in which I sought safety and sanctuary. I felt my muscles turn to steel and it was if someone poured ice water through my soul. At times, the depth of rage, betrayal and pain seemed all consuming and I never knew a body or heart could produce so many tears."

Here is some of that *creative adventure* under hypnosis:

Therapist: Where are you?

Athena: I'm not born yet...I'm with people that I feel really safe with...that I really love a lot...some of them are teachers, and they are showing me....

Therapist: What are they showing you?

Athena: They are showing me where I'm going to be going and what some of my opportunities are...I don't think I'm going to like being down there....

Therapist: What kind of things are they showing you?

Athena: They are showing me that there is going to be a family and I'm going to be part of this family and there are going to be some situations that are going to be really hard and trying.

Therapist: How do you feel about that?

*Athena: Well...I know—I just know it's going to be pretty hard and they're showing me...almost like on this film strip and I'm seeing my life and it starts to take shape and form and I'm seeing what **can** be and what **might** be, but it is going to depend on how I perceive to learn from it and it's just...oh, boy, there is a feeling coming into my body....*

Therapist: How does it feel?

Athena: I feel kind of like this pull and I think it it's getting time to go—

Therapist: To go where?

Athena: Into the body...inside my mother and...it feels so different here...oh...I don't think I want to do this....

Athena continues, "The illusion of separation—what I wanted to understand was—*why* did I create this experience? Dr. Peebles told me that I had made a decision to leave the body in the form of an accident but he and my teachers intervened and I decided to stay in the body and confront the issue. He said I chose the experience as a form of self-punishment and that I wanted to be bold about it and to experience it in very dynamic terms, that I didn't want to be shy about it or put it off. It stemmed, he told me, from a life as a prostitute and in that life, I had judged myself severely.

"He said, 'Your society operates under a massive illusion of victimhood and to most, the idea that a soul would choose such an experience is revolting, repugnant and disgusting. What has been most difficult for you, Athena, is how you looked at it as a *child* rather than a *soul*, so think of it in terms of a soul *choosing* to accelerate their growth. The one who has chosen the experience is seeking to *increase* their communication concerning their sexuality. The perpetrator or abuser is operating from *decreased* communication concerning their sexuality. So you see, my dear, the two serve each other.'

"Now I understood why I felt such empathy toward prostitutes. Just a few weeks earlier, I had considered doing some volunteer work in that arena. Shortly after I completed my work with Dr. Slavin, I had an experience that to this day still leaves me shaking my head in complete amazement.

"A prostitute, dazed, defeated and confused, walked directly up to me as I was coming out of a store in Marina del Rey, California. I had thought it highly unusual for she was completely out of her element. 'Are you a spiritual woman,' she asked. 'Yes,' I replied somewhat hesitantly, 'what's the matter?' In one fragile breath she told me, 'I'm a prostitute. I'm running away from my pimp and I'm going to kill myself.' I suggested a woman's shelter and her reply was, 'He knows where they are…he'll kill me.' She then recounted for me the horrible ways that he had punished her physically. She then mumbled, 'I need to find a church. I need to go to Texas, I have a friend there…a church, maybe they can get me a ticket. Are you a spiritual woman?'

"The shop owner had stood listening wide-eyed and watched in disbelief as I put the woman in my car. I drove around looking for a church and listened as she began to describe crazy parallels between her childhood and mine. It seemed a different time and place, *surreal*, and I felt as if I were part of a Salvador Dali painting, some abstract symbol melting down a side of a mountain. *Ah, to hell with it,* I thought as I pulled into a travel agency and whipped out my credit card. One hundred and seventy eight dollars later I dropped this poor decrepit creature off in front of United Airlines. I knew she was telling the truth. Whether or not she got on the plane, I don't know and it's not important. What was important was that something inside me *had* to respond. Dr. Peebles later confirmed that the act of kindness was an act of forgiveness to the prostitute of my past life, and this act had released the remaining karma associated with it. Magical."

◆   ◆   ◆

Athena now tells us of how she sees that loving allowance for all things to be in their own time and space starting with herself, has manifested in her life.

"At the sharing of my story in *To Dance With Angels*, I had self-righteously claimed that I had forgiven my mother. The truth of the matter was that I felt a sense of relief at her passing. I felt as if a diseased portion of my life had been cut out and removed and I was so damned angry that she wouldn't take any responsibility for her part in allowing this perpetrator into our lives. Even a little acknowledgment would have helped. I felt as if all of this was dumped in my lap to resolve however I could. That infuriated me but underneath it all was a whole lot of hurt. I needed the space and the allowance after her death to simply let things settle and move into the next phase of healing naturally.

"What I learned for myself was that I had to allow of my emotions the thunder and the lightning, the sadness, loss and grief their equal time, their equal space, and to allow them to be exactly what they were—raw, passionate and real. I couldn't bypass the anger at Point A and jump to forgiveness, Point Z, without moving through them. To do so was nothing more than an empty affirmation. *I forgive you. I forgive you. I forgive you with my head but not my heart.* I read once if you can't forgive, you can't forget, and if you can't forget you can't forgive.

"Shortly after her death, I asked Dr. Peebles how she was doing. He said, 'She is constantly wiping her brow with the back of her hand.'(as she did in life) 'She wants to go back and live her life backwards. In other words, spirit is telling her that she lived her life exactly as she had to.'

"I'm not sure exactly when the shift began to happen but I know that when I thought of Mom, my feelings felt softer, somehow. I inquired how my mother was doing of medium Ron Smith. The reply was, 'She weeps much in her slumber.' I felt such a wave of sadness flood through my body. Those words broke my heart.

"I found myself reflecting back to the time in which under hypnosis I experienced my time in spirit prior to this incarnation. The feeling of awareness and clarity, of safety and love, expanded vision of a grander overview and the ability to see before me opportunities to be gained or missed. How great my mother's pain and disappointment in self to see where she had detached herself out of fear and pain and to view the rejection response of her child, a soul to whom she had given birth. How great her pain. She weeps much in her slumber.

"One of the greatest gifts my mother ever gave me came in the form of contact through a very gifted medium and internationally recognized channeling teacher, Shawn Randall. Torah, a non-physical multi-dimensional consciousness channeled by Shawn, agreed to help set the stage for this communication to take place. I listened in anticipation as Torah began to make the connection and lovingly coaxed my mother forward reassuring her that she was safe, that it was okay to enter this dimension, to feel the love present in the room, and that this could help to heal her as well. I watched in amazement as the medium began to hyperventilate and to grab at her heart just as my mother always did in life. I placed my hand upon her heart and spoke to my mother. I felt as if *I* were the mother and *she* was the child, unsure, scared and vulnerable, *yet willing*, despite *her fears*, to re-enter a dimension that represented so much pain for her. She didn't deny me…she acknowledged me. That meant more to me than I can ever convey through paper or pen.

"Later that evening the medium told me that for a week prior to our meeting she kept repeating, 'Who's Olivia? Who's Olivia?' Olivia is my mother.

"To truly forgive my mother meant letting go of the illusion of victimhood. That was scary. What would I blame my own inadequacies on? I couldn't blame any failures on my childhood, or lack thereof, I couldn't blame my unwillingness to engage or embrace life on him, her, or circumstances. To be free is a choice of the moment.

"I went to my mother's grave in February of 1998. There I sat on the grass and spoke to her of my discovery, insights gained, my healing, and about my new-found enthusiasm for life. I reflected upon her many beautiful qualities, her sacred reverence for nature, her love of poetry and gift of pen, her silent quest for God, and her ability to find humor in conditions that at times seemed utterly deplorable. I know now that she did the best she could. Her denial was so great that her pain would have engulfed her. *That*, she feared the most, and I can understand that.

"What I so deeply wanted to convey to her was for her to *feel* within her consciousness how much I desired for her to be free without self-judgement or condemnation. We both had suffered enough. It was time. I opened my heart and felt the love; I visualized the light surrounding her, penetrating and healing her spirit. Christ once said forgive actually means *give for* those who are incapable of giving. In giving *for* my Mom, I gave *for* myself a new beginning.

"Next to her picture, pressed between glass and paper is a flower from her grave, an echo to my own soul, and an oracle of wisdom stated so eloquently:

> *'To be born again is to let the past go, and look without condemnation upon the present.'*
>
> —*A Course in Miracles.*

"I must say in all honesty that the sharing of my experience leaves me feeling somewhat naked and vulnerable. That, however, is okay, it just feels new.

"In closing I would like to share a message that was given for me by *Almak*, one of my guides, through Dr. Peebles. Now, years later, I fully comprehend, not in logic, but in resonance, the meaning of the following words: '*Athena, you are a light bearer and as you step forward with your gift of light to the world, first you must know the darkness and the shadows of your own, and in knowing the same, you will discover the desire not only to honor and to kneel before those dark places but to see them as beautiful and divine because of your willingness to be transformed through that darkness into the light.'* To begin anew."

Thank you, Athena, for again sharing. I am sure there are many who will read your words and identify in countless ways with them. I pray, as I know you do, that it will give them hope and courage and the knowing that there *are* endings and new beginnings. And, God bless that child who is safe and secure within your heart.

15

THE CREATIVE DANCE

"Look forward to change, and you will know happiness.
Resist the same, and you will know pain."

—*The grand spirit, Dr. Peebles*

Athena has just illustrated for us the incredible power of forgiveness. We have also seen how the opportunity to forgive does not end when someone dies, as Dr. Peebles has pointed out. Our love and our thoughts have the capability of piercing through the veil that separates our world and the world of spirit. The opportunity for forgiveness to occur comes through communication such as prayer, meditation, within dreams, by journaling, and with messages that come through the gift of mediumship.

But most importantly, true forgiveness occurs within at the heart level not at the mind level. It is the opening up of the heart which allows for loving allowance to enter and express fully. And as Dr. Peebles impresses upon us, it has to begin with self. It is only then that it will be free to move outward and beyond.

So often when someone passes to the other side the living are left with regrets and unexpressed feelings—things that should have been said and weren't, forgiveness that was never given by one or both, and even unexpressed anger. Often, the grieving person longs for one more chance to communicate, to make things right in their own mind. They may feel over-burdened with guilt, incomplete, distressed. By allowing those emotions to be expressed through prayer, meditation, the written word, regrets can be overcome and forgiveness can manifest. We regain our power as we become a whole and complete spiritual being again.

If we can take Dr. Peebles' spiritual psychology to heart, integrate the teachings into our lives, acknowledge that we are the creator of our life adventure, understand that we are here for lessons which we have fashioned and designed for our own soul growth, take responsibility, and come from loving allowance in all its entirety, then we can experience an extraordinary emancipation. Life, each and everyday, presents us with choices. How do we perceive those choices? Do we see problems and difficulties as challenges to be solved and overcome or do we see them fearfully as disabling, immobilizing and defeating? When we realize that we are not victims, that our perceptions of life belong to us and to us alone, that we have choice to design the intricacies of our world within our individual mind, we become free. And it is within that freedom that we respond to life in a loving and charitable way.

Life is never stagnate. It is in constant motion, and the movement may not always be to our liking, but within that movement is of course change. But in recognizing that change does take place moment to moment, we have the choice to respond in any way we wish. And that is freedom.

We are on a cosmic journey, one that has no ending, yet is filled with new beginnings. We hold the power within ourselves to enable those new beginnings to foster and advance our personal spiritual development.

In our own hand we hold the key to happiness. The door begins to open when we have found the God connection and the self connection. When we love our self, are comfortable with who we are and our place within the universe, nothing else really matters because it matters not that we do not have the approval of another, are not considered successful, are not appreciated. By being centered and functioning from our innermost self, we attract the abundance of life to us, but do not depend on it for happiness and joy. It enriches us, yes, but it is not the sustenance of life because that is within. Happiness is ours, if we choose for it to be ours. When we come from that place of wholeness, victimhood drops away, neediness vanishes, as does dependance, and are all replaced by inner-strength, self-worth, and a sense of empowerment.

In a healthy human life we have the desire to be loved, to communicate, to be appreciated, to have joy and pleasure, and to *give* those things as well as receive them. But there is an enormous difference between desiring these things in our life and being so dependant on others to "supply" these things. When one cannot find fulfillment within, then one tends to look outward and often sacrifices a big part of themselves in the frantic hunt to fill those needs. And often, what is discovered is emptiness as the longing for self grows.

Dr. Peebles will share some additional wisdom with us on how easily we can achieve spiritual enhancement within. It all begins with the most powerful of his principles, the foundation of the three principles, loving allowance.

Dr. Peebles: God bless each and every one. It is our pleasure and joy to communicate with you in regards to the journey of spiritual growth. With each moment each of you move closer to enlightenment and oneness with God. It is a delightful journey, one filled with creative adventure and delightful, yes, delightful opportunities.

Now in the study of the three principles, what are you calling them Linda—three principles of angelic wisdom—rightfully named, as they do come from the angels—in some ways beyond Dr. Peebles here. They have become an important part of my philosophy as I have observed human nature from this side and, of course, from your side. In order to move upward, closer to God, one first has to understand that there is, indeed, no separation from God. Not at all. God is ever present, in all things, in the light and shadows, in all movement. When one comes to that understanding, that God is all, that each of you is a part of the all, in other words a part of God, then how can any separation be? So with that understanding, that you are a part of God, that represents the love of God, does it not? So if God loves, then man loves, right? Who does God love? You. Love is ever so powerful. It is unconditional.

The illusion of separation can cloud not only your view of God but your view of yourself as a spiritual being—a spiritual being who deserves love and because you already have the love of God, (whether you know that or not) then the rest is up to you. You have the choice and the power within your very soul to love your *self.* Yes. To love God is also to love *you.*

Now, when you arrive at that understanding and have loving allowance starting with yourself, then at that time the movement of love really begins. It flowers, it radiates, and it embraces all of life.

We have spoken of how difficult it can be come to the understanding that you are worthy, and so on, but listen up; not only are you worthy of God's love but you are worthy of your own love. Oh, yes, often others will try to convince you that you are not worthy but that is just an aspect of their own illusion of separation talking. So allow them, with love, their point of view; hear it, respect it, but then you can let it go, and proceed on with loving yourself as God loves you.

It will be a lesson for them, too, as they watch the diversity of thought in action, and possibly in some teeny tiny way it may dissolve some of their personal illusion of separation as they see you become more self-assured, more loving not only in regards to self but also to others.

They may look at you (behind your back, so to speak) and wonder how you did it. They may think, *I* could do that too. So the journey of growth continues, ever expanding. We do learn from others, no doubt, but we also learn from ourselves, Dr. Peebles here, included.

The journey of the soul is a fascinating one. It is forever full of surprises, challenges, and delights. It may have its dark places at times, but it is within the darkness that the greatest light can be discovered. Lights and shadows are of God, and are excellent opportunities of soul growth. So do not fear the shadows, for within shadows are found echoes of the soul.

When you understand that you are the pilot of your life, that you are at the controls, then life will become a journey of joy. You are in charge of your own locomotion and the natural movement of the universe, change, will not be feared. It will be welcomed as another lesson to study and learn from. But if you resist and fear change, the result will be pain.

But you say, *Dr. Peebles, I do not want change in my life.* Well, my dears, change is inevitable. It is the universal movement of the mind of God. Life is in constant eternal motion. It is that spinning of the spiral, absorbing, embracing, swirling, gathering, repelling, creating, as it dances. So learn to welcome change because within it will be found spiritual growth and enhancement.

But as you welcome change, as the creator that you are, you have the ability to move with that change in whatever way you wish. If you deny it, you will have pain. You will feel victimized, helpless. But if you embrace it then you have the opportunity to have a creative dance with it. And in that creative dance you can mold it, fashion it, to your own liking. If you want it to be an opportunity for new experiences, so be it. If you want it to be adventurous, so be it. If you want it to be mysterious, so be it. And if you want it to be denied, so be it.

It is your ballet slippers that move across the stage, it is your melody that is strummed on the musical instruments, and it is your audience who experiences your song and dance. You are the choreographer, the composer, the arranger, the director. It is your show and you decide how you want to present it. But might I suggest, dear friends, that you hold no expectations of how others will receive it—just present it with an open mind and loving heart. And present it with joy!

Linda: Thank you.

◆   ◆   ◆

In Western cultures there appears to be much resistance to the idea of reincarnation. Many do believe that we are immortal, but to allow for that immortality to have a beginning in previous lives, before our birth into this life, is difficult for many to accept. But the belief in reincarnation, most commonly associated with certain Eastern cultures and religions, is not only an ancient belief but has been widespread throughout the world. Modern scholars have discovered that the idea had wide favor throughout the early Americas, both North and South, in Europe, and persisted into the Christian Era. Scholars can point to many examples of early Christian and Jewish thought centered around the idea of re-birth. Apparently the early Christians, somehow threatened by the idea of rebirth or reincarnation for the common man, had most references to it removed from the Bible.

Many of our more-contemporary great thinkers, philosophers, noted writers and poets, educators, and scientists have acknowledged reincarnation as the most sensible paradigm for human immortality. And the shift of paradigm in the Western world appears to be gaining momentum as evidence to support the idea comes forward from various avenues of serious study. It is an idea that will benefit from more exploration.

For myself, it has been part of my belief system for as long as I can remember. It just seemed to be logical and reasonable and a part of spiritual reality. Proof? I personally don't need any more than I already have gathered in my experiences and research. To me it is a fact of life. In some ways, I am still that young girl of seven or eight that *knew* I had been here before, and in all probability, would be again. Many of my experiences throughout life have only confirmed the fact for me. Especially Don, with the incredible love bond we had; knowing, recognizing each other the moment our eyes met across a room; and always *knowing* each other in the deepest sense of the word throughout our years together. Soulmates, you bet. And, also, especially my experiences with Dr. Peebles.

So is reincarnation part of our creative dance? I think so. Dr. Peebles tells us it is from his home on the spirit side.

But he also wrote about the knowing of another soul in his book, *Seers of the Ages*. He penned, "Souls require no introduction. The recognition is intuitional. Meeting a noble soul that knows our soul, we indulge the pleasing truth to us, that we knew the loved one in a pre-existent state, and delicious were those delicate experiences in the sweet realms of blessedness."

Pre-existent state? Might I ask, where and when and in what form? A soul is a soul, is it not?—whether wrapped in the garment of the current physical dimension, or the etheric finery of the other dimension, or the garment of a past life that is delicately hidden away in the recesses of the soul's mind only to come forward in new and subtle awareness from time to time throughout the eternal journey.

The creative dance of the spiritual self personifies a succession of endings and new beginnings which go on throughout our human life—and forevermore.

But we are always filled with wonder—What is life all about? Who are we? Why are we here? Does life truly go on? When a loved one passes from the body and continues on their own journey, it feels very much like they have left us behind. But have they? Are they really out of our reach? Those answers are found inside our hearts, in our experiences, in our faith, and in the understanding that we are spiritual beings, only encased in a physical body for a short period of time.

Dr. Peebles wrote in his 1880 book, *Immortality*, "The soul is ever a questioner. From its earliest recorded experiences it has interrogated itself and the surrounding universe for a solution of the mystery of its being and the momentous changes that necessarily await it."

The creative dance is a dance of change and new beginnings.

16

CELEBRATION

"It is the paradoxes of life that can be studied to understand higher truth."

—*The grand spirit, Dr. Peebles*

Dr. Peebles will often tell us that we need to lighten up and not take life so seriously. Those words of course do not mean that we should not be responsible and live our lives in the best way that we can, but to understand that we are doing the best we can at any given moment and that all our experiences and our responses to those experiences are just part of our lessons and growth as we journey through life.

By utilizing the three principles of angelic wisdom offered to us by Dr. Peebles, our lives can become more joyous, more enriched, more satisfying. By integrating the principles into our consciousness they become spontaneous, second nature to us. Obviously, we may sometimes fail in our efforts to put the principles fully into use with every situation that presents itself, but they do become a way of thinking and responding—a new way at looking at life and at ourselves.

If we are able to shed the illusion of separation, to increase our capacity and ability to love, to recognize the fundamental goodness in others and in ourselves, to appreciate that we are all spiritual beings, and to look forward to life as a creative adventure, then most of the trials and tribulations that life can present become lighter, less fearful and threatening, and much easier to overcome.

As you begin to fully understand the three principles, and the illusion of separation and fear of intimacy, you can then start to focus on your true mission in life, not a mission for the world at large, (except in the ultimate sense), but a mission for yourself, your own growth, your own image of self. You become lighter, joyous, and your life will overflow with expressions of love as you put the principles into action and reaction. Life becomes a celebration.

Let's see what Dr. Peebles has to say about the celebration of life.

Dr. Peebles: God bless you each and every one. You are each embarked on a journey of love to the heart, and in that journey you will find the essence of your soul as you surrender to the delightful opportunities of growth which await you. Life *is* a celebration, a dance of joy to be sure. You came to Planet Earth for many lessons, most designed by self, to ensure that you will grow, will have spiritual enrichment and new understandings of self.

As you come to understand your purpose, your journey of love, and to dissolve the illusion of separation—from God, from self and from others—you will find joy beyond your wildest dreams and imagination.

Contained within the foundation of the three principles is the key. Love is at the foundation and as you build upon that foundation, you will discover freedom in the expression of self. As you recognize that you are a spiritual being on a journey toward higher understanding, a movement toward the God-essence and ultimately, God, you will discover what a joyous sojourn you are embarked upon.

As you embrace the three principles, you embrace love. Not a superficial love, but a heart and soul felt love—the pure essence of love. And it is in that full expression of love where you will find the meaning of eternal existence.

Your journey this time on Earth is only a brief journey within the whole of existence, but is an important journey filled with wonderful opportunities to learn more about self, and in doing so, to learn more about others. Earth is a study in relationships, the relationship with God, with self, with your fellow humans, with nature, and also with the world of spirit.

When one understands that there is no death, only change; that there is always access to the spirit world—your home to which you will return at some point; that never are you alone nor unloved; that you are the creator of your dance of life and it is you who holds the paint brush to stroke your canvas in any way you wish; that your innate fears of intimacy can be mastered; that separation from God, from self, from others, from spirit, is only an illusion; then you will celebrate with joy the dance of life.

We, in the spirit world, rejoice when we are able to give guidance. We are always available to assist you on your journey, to present a point of view which may enable you to see more clearly, to reassure you that you are not alone, especially at your darkest moments. All you have to do is call upon us, the angels, the messengers, whose pleasure it is to convey to you the love of God.

For myself, Dr. Peebles, it is my greatest joy and pleasure to commune with you. I present to you the wisdom and often, the humor, which in some way, may make your journey to the heart and soul a little easier, a little lighter. It is an honor for me to be joined by the others on this side, and to be able to bring forward to each of you our spiritual psychology. Embrace the principles and you will embrace love. Embrace love and you will know God. Know God and you will know All.

Lighten up and enjoy life. Celebrate, celebrate, for life is a joy, it really is. And as you grow, may you grow in love.

Go your ways in peace, love, and harmony as you remember who you are—a spiritual being. Peace and love begin within. You can know harmony as you respect and love the differences, not only in yourself but in the world around you. It has been our delight to dance the dance of angels in celebration of life.

God bless you each and every one.

17

AND THE BEAT GOES ON

o o o o o o o o o o o o o o o o o o o o o o o o o o o o o
"Invisible guests walk by our sides, witness our toils and
struggles and listen in sadness or rapture to the breathing
words that drop from our lips."

—James Martin Peebles, 1890

Within these pages I have presented a look at the remarkable terrestrial
life of James Martin Peebles. Dr. Peebles is one of the few spirit entities
in communication from the other side whose life can be traced, and in
turn, show the comparisons, the parallels, of who he was while on earth
and who he is on the spirit side. I'm sure you have seen that his personality, his consciousness, lives on. While here on Earth for nearly a hundred years, he was on a mission to spread his spiritual message, a
message centered around love, compassion and humanity. His current
mission, now from the other side, remains the same. Is this not extraordinary and phenomenal?

I recall that Dr. Peebles mentioned several years ago that before long
the time would come when communication with spirit would be common and many of us would often be able to see spirit. Either people are
having more mystical experiences than ever before, or are just more
open to talking about those experiences because there does seem to be
an increase of communion in various forms. Is the veil between worlds
becoming thinner? Is multi dimensionality becoming more understood? Are we on the verge of a new (or renewed) spiritual awareness,

quite in contrast to the social ills which plague us? Is the pendulum about to swing back toward a sense of community? And will it swing in time to save humanity from destroying itself? Will the influence of the spirit world help us to set things right? It probably will, if we listen, if we do all we can do to spread *love*.

As James admitted in many of his writings, his message was inspired by spirit guides—his band of angels. Within his earthly writings was a gift of great wisdom and compassion. Many years ago, before most of those reading this incarnated, he moved on to the other side where he became leader of the band. Now, as spokesman for his band of angels, Dr. Peebles shares pearls of angelic wisdom. Those of us who are lucky enough to have contact with Dr. Peebles, either directly or through the written word, are recipients of a great offering of love. The spiritual psychology which Dr. Peebles so lovingly shares with us has the ability to change our lives and enhance our spiritual growth in tremendous ways. For many it can be life-changing, as you have read within this book. His practical, down-to-earth advice can be so easily applied and it comes to us in three very understandable principles:

1. Loving Allowance for all things to be in their own time and place, beginning with yourself.

2. Increased Communication with all of life everywhere, and with respect.

3. Self Responsibility, for you are the eternal creator, never the victim.

Think of the wisdom of these principles as a thirty day spiritual-enriching diet. Try incorporating them into your life for the next thirty days and see what happens. See if not your very soul and heart feel fuller, more nourished, more complete. By the end of the thirty days you should feel lighter as you dump the garbage, refreshed as you regain your personal power, and peaceful and content as you know that you are not alone and are connected in a true sense to God, to yourself, and to your fellow man. I believe that you will find that this diet of spiritual enrichment will be the soul sustenance that you have been searching for all your life. And with this diet you have nothing to lose, but what you have to gain is the *celebration of self.*

As the band of angels play for us their heavenly melodies, sing your songs and dance with the angels in celebration.

The band plays on, the beat goes on....

ABOUT THE AUTHOR

Linda Pendleton is author of *A Walk Through Grief: Crossing the Bridge Between Worlds,* and *Three Principles of Angelic Wisdom: The Spiritual Psychology of the Grand Spirit, Dr. Peebles. Three Principles of Angelic Wisdom* was awarded the EPPIE 2000 Best Nonfiction Award in the Philosophy/Spiritual Category, given for the finest in E-books. *Three Principles of Angelic Wisdom* is a follow-up book to the popular book, *To Dance With Angels, An Amazing Journey to the Heart with the Phenomenal Thomas Jacobson and the Grand Spirit, Dr. Peebles,* co-written with her husband, novelist, Don Pendleton.

Linda is coauthor with Don Pendleton of *Whispers From the Soul: The Divine Dance of Consciousness, The Metaphysics of the Novel: The Inner Workings of a Novel and a Novelist,* and the novel, *One Dark and Stormy Night...the Search for the Sunrise Killer. One Dark and Stormy*

Night was an EPPIE 2001 Finalist in the Best Thriller Category. The book has been retitled, *Roulette*.

Linda also writes screenplays and Comic book adaptations and has designed a line of angel cards.

You can learn more about Linda Pendleton at her web site: **http:// www.todancewithangels.com**

BIBLIOGRAPHY AND SUGGESTED READING

Altea, Rosemary. *The Eagle and the Rose*. New York: Warner Books, 1995.

_____. *Proud Spirit*. New York: William Morrow, 1997.

Anderson, George, and Andrew Barone. *Lessons From the Light*. New York: G. P. Putnam's Sons, 1999.

Barrett, Joseph O. *The Spiritual Pilgrim, A Biography of James M. Peebles*. Boston: W. White & Company, 1872.

Bernstein, Morey. *The Search For Bridey Murphy*. New York: Doubleday & Company, 1956.

Brinkley, Dannion, with Paul Perry. *Saved by the Light*. New York: Villard Books/Random House, 1994.

_____*At Peace in the Light*. New York: Harper Collins, 1995.

Browne, Sylvia. *The Other Side and Back*. New York: Dutton, 1999.

Dossey, Larry. *Recovering the Soul: A Scientific and Spiritual Search*. New York: Bantam Books, 1989.

_____. *Healing Words*. San Francisco: HarperSan Francisco, 1993.

Eadie, Betty J. *Embraced by the Light*. Placerville, California: Gold Leaf Press, 1992. New York: Bantam, 1994.

Edward, John. *One Last Time*. New York: Berkley Books, 1998.

_____. *Crossing Over*. San Diego, California: Jodere Group, Inc., 2001.

Guggenheim, Bill, and Judy Guggenheim. *Hello From Heaven!* New York: Bantam Books, 1996.

Head, Joseph, and S. L. Cranston. *Reincarnation: The Phoenix Fire Mystery*. New York: Julian Press, 1977.

Klimo, Jon. *Channeling*. Los Angeles: Jeremy P. Tarcher, 1987.

Kubis, Pat, and Mark Macy. *Conversations Beyond the Light with Departed Friends & Colleagues by Electronic Means*. Boulder, Colorado: Griffen Publishing in association with Continuing Life Research, 1995.

Kübler-Ross, Elisabeth. *On Death and Dying*. New York: Macmillan, 1969.

_____. *On Children and Death*. New York: Macmillan, 1983.

_____. *Death: The Final Stage of Growth*. New York: Simon & Schuster, 1975.

_____. *AIDS: The Ultimate Challenge*. New York: Macmillan, 1987.

_____. *Questions and Answers on Death and Dying*. New York: Macmillan, 1974.

_____. *The Wheel of Life: A Memoir of Living and Dying*. New York: Scribner, 1997.

Martin, Joel, and Patricia Romanowski. *We Don't Die*. New York: G. P. Putnam's Sons, 1988.

_____. *We Are Not Forgotten*. New York: G. P. Putnam's Sons, 1991.

_____. *Our Children Forever*. New York: Berkley Books, 1994.

Moody, Raymond. *Life After Life*. New York: Bantam Books, 1975.

Moody, Raymond, with Paul Perry. *Reunions*. New York: Villard Books, 1990.

Morrissey, Diane. *Anyone Can See the Light*. Walpole, New Hampshire: Stillpoint Publishing, 1996.

Morse, Melvin, with Paul Perry. *Closer to the Light*. New York: Villard Books, 1990.

_____. *Transformed by the Light*. New York: Villard Books, 1992.

_____. *Parting Visions*. New York: Villard Books, 1994.

Peebles, James Martin. *Immortality*. Boston: Colby and Rich, 1880, 1890.

_____. *Seers of the Ages, Spiritualism Past and Present*. Boston: W. White and Company, 1869; Chicago: Progressive Thinker Publishing, 1903.

Pendleton, Don, and Linda Pendleton. *To Dance With Angels*. New York: Zebra Books, 1990, 1992; Pinnacle Books, 1995; Kensington, 1996.

Rodegast, Pat, and Judith Stanton. *Emmanuel's Book*. New York: Friend's Press, 1985.

_____. *Emmanuel's Book II*. New York: Bantam Books, 1989.

_____. *Emmanuel's Book III*. New York: Bantam Books, 1994.

Roman, Sanaya, and Duane Packer. *Opening to Channel*. Tiburon, California: H. J. Kramer, 1987.

Schwartz, Gary E., and William L. Simon. *The AfterLife Experiments*. New York: Pocket Star, 2002.

Sugrue, Thomas. *There is a River*. New York: Henry Holt and Company, 1943. Virginia Beach, Virginia: A.R.E. Press, 1973.

Van Praagh, James. *Talking to Heaven*. New York: Dutton Books, 1997.

_____. *Reaching to Heaven*. New York: Dutton Books, 1999.

_____. *Healing Grief*. New York: Dutton Books, 2000.

Weiss, Brian. *Many Lives, Many Masters*. New York: Simon & Schuster, 1988.

_____. *Through Time Into Healing*. New York: Simon & Schuster, 1992.

_____. *Only Love is Real: A Story of Soulmates Reunited*. New York: Warner Books, 1996.

Whipple, Edward. *A Biography of James M. Peebles, M.D., A.M.* Battle Creek, Mich.: self-published, 1901.

Zukav, Gary. *The Seat of the Soul.* New York: Simon and Schuster, 1989.

0-595-26274-0

8842343R0

Made in the USA
Lexington, KY
07 March 2011